A Taste of Asia

A Culinary Journey Through the Flavors of the East

Malai Saelim

Table of Contents

Introduction

Welcome to the world of Asian soups and Thai recipes! This cookbook is a celebration of the vibrant and diverse flavors of the East. From the rich and spicy broths of

Ramen Chicken Noodle to the delicate and comforting miso soups of Japan, you'll find an array of dishes that are sure to tantalize your taste buds. Whether you're a seasoned chef or just starting out, this cookbook offers something for everyone, with simple and easy-to-follow recipes that are perfect for any occasion. So, grab a spoon and join us on a culinary journey through the delicious soups and dishes of Asia and Thailand.

Recipes

Thailand's Famous Poultry Curry

This decadent Thai chicken curry is very easy to prepare and cook for the entire family. You may add more chilis for hotter dish. And you can add left-over turkey or meat from last night's dinner.

Ingredients:

Main ingredients

3-5 cups chicken, cut into 2" squares

2 cups left-over turkey or meat, chopped

2 cups toasted croutons or bread slices, cubed

½ cup corn oil

1 small white onions, chopped

2 cloves garlic, chopped

1 tsp chopped celery stick

2 stalks fresh young lemongrass

1 cup sweet potatoes, roasted and cut into cubes 2"

½ cup fresh bamboo shoots, wash and drained

1 medium red bell pepper, cored and cubed 1"

1 medium yellow bell pepper, cored and cubed 1"

2 fresh kaffir lime leaves

2 fresh bay leaves

1 cup tomato sauce

2 cups coconut milk

1 tbsp coconut vinegar

Special Curry Sauce:

3 red chilis

½ tsp cayenne pepper

1 small red onion, peeled

2 tbsp fresh ginger, peeled

½ tsp powdered cumin

¼ tsp powdered sage

¼ tsp powdered anise seed

¼ tsp freshly grated nutmeg

a dash of cinnamon

a dash of curry powder

½ cup light soy sauce

½ cup fish sauce

1 tbsp shrimp paste

3 tbsp brown sugar

Directions:

In a big casserole sauté the onions, garlic, ginger and celery for 3 minutes or until soft. Add the cut-up chicken meat and sauté until it turns white. Add all the main ingredients and simmer for 20 minutes.

Puree all the curry sauce ingredients in a blender and pulse for 20 seconds. OR You may chop and pound in a mortar and pestle. Set aside and cover.

Stir to combine the curry mixture with the main ingredients in the casserole. Simmer more for 5 minutes. Remove the lemongrass before transferring to a serving bowl.

Serving suggestion:

Serve hot with steamed rice or French bread. This dish goes well with either a milkshake or a fruit smoothie to counter the spiciness.

Skewered Thai Treats

This delicious Thai skewered dish is very easy to prepare and cook for the kids. It's packed with vitamins and nutrients. This recipe is good for 5 treats.

Ingredients:

Main ingredients

2 cups chicken, cut into 2" squares

5 bacon strips

5 pcs firm tofu, quartered

10 pcs button mushrooms

10 pcs pineapple cubes

1 medium yellow bell pepper, cored and cubed 2"

½ cup corn oil

Marinade:

1 cup coconut milk

1 tbsp lime juice

a dash of curry powder

½ cup fish sauce

1 tbsp brown sugar

Directions:

In a small casserole simmer the marinade for 10 minutes and stir until it thickens. Set aside and cover.

Prepare all the main ingredients. Skewer and pierce each ingredient. Place on a clean tray or platter. Pour the marinade. Marinate at least 1 hour before cooking, so it becomes more flavorful.

Roast or pan-fry the skewered treats until cooked. Serve immediately.

Serving suggestion:

Serve hot with steamed pandan rice or your favorite noodle dish.

Stir-fry Veggie and Beef Strips with Peanut Sauce

This delicious veggie and beef dish is very easy to prepare and cook for the family. It's packed with vitamins and nutrients.

Ingredients:

1 cup beef brisket, cut into thin strips

2 bacon strips, chopped finely

2 pcs firm tofu, quartered

1 cup snow peas, ends trimmed

5 pcs shiitake mushrooms cut into thin strips

2 pcs eggplants cut lengthwise

1 medium carrot cut lengthwise

1 medium red bell pepper, cored and julienned

½ cup tamarind juice

½ cup corn oil

1 medium white onion, sliced

3 cloves garlic, peeled and sliced

1 tsp fresh ginger, peeled and sliced

Peanut sauce:

½ cup peanut butter

½ cup truffle cream

½ cup coconut milk

2 tbsp coco jam a dash of curry powder

a dash of salt and pepper

Toppings:

1 tsp chopped fresh chives

1 tsp roasted sesame seeds

Directions:

In a small casserole simmer the peanut sauce for 10 minutes and stir until it thickens. Set aside and cover.

In as separate casserole, heat the corn oil - Sauté the onions, ginger and garlic for 3 minutes. Add the beef and bacon, sauté for 5 minutes. Mix in the tamarind juice and let it simmer until juice evaporated. Add in all the vegetable ingredients and simmer for 3 minutes.

Pour over the peanut sauce and simmer for 5 minutes more. Serve immediately and topped with chives and sesame seeds.

Serving suggestion:

Serve hot as rice toppings or on your favorite noodles.

Stir-fry Veggie, Fruits and Pork Strips with Coconut Sauce

It's a delicious veggie and pork dish, very easy to prepare and cook for the unexpected guests.

Ingredients:

2 cups pork tenderloin, cut into thin strips

1 cup chorizo sausages cut into thin strips

2 pcs firm tofu, sliced into rectangular pieces

1 cup snow peas, ends trimmed

1 cup oyster mushrooms cut into half

½ cup pineapple tidbits

½ cup red apples, cubed 1"

½ cup leeks cut into thin rings

½ cup tamarind juice

½ cup vegetable oil

1 medium white onion, sliced

2 cloves garlic, peeled and sliced

1 tsp fresh ginger, peeled and sliced

1 tsp fresh red chilli pepper, chopped

Coconut sauce:

1 cup coconut milk

2 tbsp coco jam

2 tbsp cornstarch

½ cup cold water

a dash of curry powder

a dash of salt and pepper

Toppings:

½ cup roasted desiccated coconut

1 tbsp chopped red chilis

Directions:

In a small bowl mix the cold water with cornstarch. Set aside.

In a small casserole simmer the coconut milk and other ingredients for 5 minutes and stir until it thickens. Add in the slurry and stir. Set aside and cover.

In as separate casserole, heat the corn oil- sauté the onions, ginger, chilli and garlic for 3 minutes. Add the pork and sausages, sauté for 5 minutes. Mix in the tamarind juice, fruits and all the vegetable ingredients. Stir and simmer for 5 minutes.

Pour over the coconut sauce and simmer for 5 minutes more. Serve immediately and topped with desiccated coconut and red chilis.

Serving suggestion:

Serve hot as rice toppings or on your favorite noodles. It may go well as pairings with fresh green salad or soup.

Thai Vegetable Soup with Chicken and Eggs

It's a delicious veggie and chicken soup, very easy to prepare and cook well as one-dish meal.

Ingredients:

2 cups chicken breast fillets, cut into thin strips

2 pcs chorizo sausages cut into thin strips

2 pcs bacon strips, chopped

1 cup chicken liver, roasted and cut into thin strips

1/2 cup garbanzos, boiled and drained

1 cup shiitake mushrooms cut into strips

12 pcs shelled quail eggs

6 chicken eggs, shelled

¼ cup leeks cut into thin rings

½ cup tamarind juice

6 cups chicken stock

½ cup vegetable oil

1 large white onion, chopped

2 cloves garlic, peeled and chopped

1 tsp fresh ginger, peeled and thinly sliced

1 tsp fresh red chilli pepper, chopped

a dash of salt and pepper

¼ cup fish sauce

Toppings:

¼ cup roasted garlic

¼ cup chopped chives

1 tbsp chopped red chilis

¼ cup fish flakes, pan-fried

Directions:

In a big casserole heat the corn oil- sauté the onions, ginger, chilli and garlic for 3 minutes. Add the chicken, bacon, liver and sausages, sauté for 5 minutes. Mix in the tamarind juice, stock, vegetables and all the ingredients. Stir and simmer for 20 minutes.

Transfer to serving bowl. Put the toppings.

Serving suggestion:

Serve hot with your favorite rice or macaroni salad.

Beef Brisket with Root Vegetables Stew

It's a delicious veggie and beef brisket stew, very easy to prepare and cook. It's tastier when reheated.

Ingredients:

3 cups beef brisket, cut into cubes 2"

3 pcs ham, sliced into thin strips

1 cup beef liver, roasted and cut into thin strips

1 cup beef innards, roasted and cut into thin strips

1 cup sweet potatoes cut into wedges

1 cup baby potatoes, washed and drained

1 cup carrots, peeled and cubed

1 cup shiitake mushrooms cut into strips

5 pcs beefsteak tomatoes, quartered

1 stalk fresh lemongrass bulb

¼ cup leeks cut into thin rings

12 pcs shelled quail eggs

½ cup tamarind juice

1 cup coconut milk

6 cups beef stock

½ cup vegetable oil

1 large white onion, chopped

2 cloves garlic, peeled and chopped

1 tsp fresh ginger, peeled and thinly sliced

1 tsp fresh red chilli pepper, chopped

a dash of salt and pepper

2 tbsp fish sauce

2 tbsp soy sauce

Toppings:

¼ cup grated Parmesan cheese

¼ minced Brie cheese

1 tbsp chopped red chilis

1 medium roasted red bell pepper, chopped

Directions:

In a big casserole heat the vegetable oil- sauté the tomatoes, onions, ginger, chilli and garlic for 3 minutes. Add the beef brisket, liver, innards and ham, sauté for 5 minutes. Mix in the tamarind juice, stock, vegetables and all the ingredients. Stir and simmer for

30 minutes. Remove the lemongrass before transferring to serving bowl.

Transfer to serving bowl. Stir in the toppings immediately so cheese melts.

Serving suggestion:

Serve hot with your favorite rice or fresh greens salad.

Salmon Fillet with Spicy Vegetable Stew

This salmon recipe is rich in flavor and packed with omega-3 fatty acids good for your heart and health. The veggie stew is packed with vitamins. This dish is delicious and easy to prepare.

Ingredients:

For the Salmon

1 whole salmon fillet, dry-rub with herbs and spices of your choice

1 tbsp corn or vegetable oil

2 tbsp lime or lemon juice

¼ tsp dried and powdered sage

¼ tsp fresh dill leaves, chopped

a dash of salt and pepper

1 pc butter stick

Vegetable mixture

1 cup sweet potatoes cut into wedges

1 cup potatoes, washed and drained

1 cup carrots, peeled and cubes 1"

1 cup button mushrooms cut into half

1 cup broccoli florets

5 pcs beefsteak tomatoes, quartered

1 stalk fresh lemongrass bulb

½ cup tamarind juice

1 cup coconut milk

½ cup vegetable oil

1 large white onion, chopped

2 cloves garlic, peeled and chopped

1 tsp fresh ginger, peeled and thinly sliced

1 tsp fresh red chilli pepper, chopped

¼ tsp cayenne powder

¼ tsp paprika

a dash of salt and pepper

½ cup oyster sauce

2 tbsp fish sauce

2 tbsp soy sauce

¼ cup grated Mozzarella cheese

1 tbsp chopped green chilis

1 medium roasted red bell pepper, chopped

Directions:

Dry rub the salmon fillet with herbs, spices and salt. Drizzle with lime or lemon juice and oil. Cover with food wrap or wax paper. Marinate at least 1 hour before cooking. (Best overnight)

Heat the frying pan with butter stick and pan fry the salmon. Turn once and cook only for 6 minutes. Transfer to serving fish platter.

In a medium casserole heat the vegetable oil- sauté the tomatoes, onions, ginger, chilli and garlic for 3 minutes. Add the root vegetables (potatoes and sweet potatoes) and sauté for 5 minutes. Mix in the tamarind juice, coconut milk, vegetables and all the ingredients. Stir and simmer for 30 minutes. Remove the lemongrass before transferring to serving dish.

Pour the vegetable stew over the fried salmon. Serve immediately.

Serving suggestion:

Serve with garlic rice or clear soup.

Seaman's Fish Cutlets
with Sweet Spicy Vegetable Casserole

This fresh fish and seafood recipe is loaded in flavor and packed with omega-3 fatty acids good for your heart. The veggie stew is packed with proteins. This dish is delicious and easy to prepare more than you think.

Ingredients:

For the fish and seafood

1 cup fresh salmon cubes 1"

1 cup fresh cod fish, deboned and cubed 1"

1 cup fresh shelled prawns, deveined

1 cup fresh clams, washed and drained

1 tbsp corn or vegetable oil

2 tbsp lime or lemon juice

¼ tsp dried thyme

¼ tsp fresh dill leaves, chopped

a dash of paprika

a dash of cayenne

a dash of salt and pepper

1 pc butter stick

Vegetable mixture

½ cup squash, peeled and cubes 1"

½ cup carrots, peeled and cubes 1"

½ cup cauliflower florets

½ cup bamboo shoots, washed and drained

½ cup cubed eggplants

3 pcs beefsteak tomatoes, quartered

1 stalk fresh lemongrass bulb

½ cup tamarind juice

2 cups coconut milk

2 tbsp vegetable oil

1 large white onion, chopped

1 tsp fresh ginger, peeled and thinly sliced

a dash of salt and pepper

a dash of turmeric powder

½ cup oyster sauce

2 tbsp fish sauce

1 tsp coriander seeds, grounded

1 tbsp chopped green chilis

3 tbsp brown sugar or molasses

Directions:

Mix the salmon, cod cubes, clams and prawns with herbs, spices and salt. Drizzle with lime or lemon juice and oil. Mix again with clean hands until seafood is covered with seasonings. Cover with food wrap or wax paper. Marinate at least 1 hour before cooking. (Best overnight)

Heat the frying pan with butter stick and pan fry the salmon, cod cubes, prawns and clams. Turn once and cook only for 8 minutes. Transfer to serving fish platter.

In a medium casserole heat the vegetable oil- sauté the tomatoes, onions, ginger, chilli and garlic for 3 minutes. Add the root vegetables (squash and carrots) and sauté for 5 minutes. Mix in the tamarind juice, coconut milk, vegetables, spices and all the ingredients. Stir and simmer for 30 minutes. Remove the lemongrass before transferring to serving dish.

Pour the vegetable stew over the fried salmon. Serve immediately.

Serving suggestion:

Serve with garlic rice or clear soup and fresh cucumber slices.

Easy Massaman Curry
with Spicy Sweet Potatoes

This beef and sweet potato stew is packed with proteins. It's delicious and easy to cook more than you think. Kids will surely ask for more servings.

Ingredients:

3 cups fresh beef brisket cubes 2"

1 cup fresh beef flanks and cubed 1"

2 cups sweet potatoes, roasted, peeled and cubed 2"

2 pcs yellow corn in a cob, cut into 3's

1 cup cherry tomatoes, roasted

1 cup red bell pepper, roasted and cubed 1"

1 cup green bell pepper, roasted and cubed 1"

3 tbsp butter

1 tbsp corn oil

1 large white onion, chopped

1 tsp fresh ginger, peeled and thinly sliced

2 tbsp lime juice

2 pcs kaffir leaves

¼ tsp dried coriander seeds

½ tsp turmeric powder a dash of paprika

a dash of salt and pepper

1 stalk fresh lemongrass bulb

1 tbsp chopped green chilis

½ cup tamarind juice

3 cups coconut milk

2 cups beef stock

3 tbsp fish sauce

3 tbsp brown sugar or molasses

Directions:

Heat the casserole with butter stick and cooking oil. Brown the beef for 5 minutes with tomatoes, onions, ginger, bell peppers, chilli and garlic.

Add the vegetables (sweet potatoes and corn) and sauté for 5 minutes. Mix in the tamarind juice, coconut milk, spices, coconut milk and all the ingredients. Stir, cover and simmer for 30 minutes in high heat (or until beef is tender). Add more beef stock to avoid drying. Remove the lemongrass before transferring to serving dish.

Transfer into big serving bowl. Serve immediately.

Serving suggestion:

Serve with steamed rice or rice noodles and fresh cucumber slices.

Grilled Thai Sate' with Sweet & Spicy Zucchinis

Kids will surely enjoy preparing these grilled meats with veggies and fruits.

Ingredients:

For Sate'

6 skewers or barbeque sticks

6 pcs fresh pork with fat, cubes 2"

6 pcs fresh chicken breast, deboned and cubed 1"

6 pcs zucchinis and cubed 2"

2 pcs yellow corn in a cob, cut into 3's

6 cherry tomatoes,

6 cubes of yellow bell pepper, cubed 1"

6 pcs cheese cubes, 1"

For marinade:

3 tbsp butter

2 tbsp annatto oil

1 tsp fresh ginger, peeled and chopped

1 tsp sugar

2 tbsp lime juice

For sauce:

1 tbsp vegetable oil

½ cup fish sauce

½ cup coconut milk

1 tbsp chopped green chilis

a dash of paprika

a dash of salt and pepper

3 tbsp brown sugar or molasses

3 tbsp peanut butter

Directions:

Mix well the marinade in deep platter. Place one by one the skewered pork, chicken and vegetables. Marinate it atleast 1 hour before cooking.

Grill the skewered treats until pork and chicken are cooked. Grill for 10-15 minutes. (Be careful not to burn the cheese and zucchinis.) Brush with the marinade.

While grilling, heat a small saucepan with butter cooking oil. Add the fish sauce, coconut milk, peanut butter and all the sauce ingredients. Simmer for 5 minutes.

Place the grilled sate' and skewered treats on a serving platter. Put the simmered sauce in small ramekins or bowls separately. Serve immediately

Serving suggestion:

Serve with steamed rice or pita bread and fresh greens salad.

Magic 7 Roasted Curry

Busy moms can easy prepare and cook this old Thai recipe with a new twist. This could be prepared in advance, freeze it and just reheat in your oven.

Ingredients:

2 cups fresh beef with fat, roasted and cut into cubes 2"

2 cups fresh beef (or pork) liver, roasted and cut into thin strips

1 cup sweet potatoes, roasted and cubed 2"

2 pcs yellow corn in a cob, roasted and cut into 3's

3 beefsteak tomatoes, roasted and quartered

1 pc large red bell pepper, roasted and cubed 2"

1 cup goat cheese, cubes 1" (any cheese would do)

1 medium chopped white onions

2 cloves chopped garlic

1 tsp fresh ginger, peeled and chopped

3 tbsp peanut butter

Juice of 1 small lime

1 tsp grated lime peel

½ cup fish sauce

3 cups coconut milk

5 pcs chopped green bird's eye chilis

1 tsp of chilli paste

1 tsp of paprika

1 tsp chopped cilantro (or coriander)

a dash of salt and pepper

3 tbsp brown sugar

For curry sauce:

1 butter stick

2 tbsp annatto oil

Directions:

Prepare the main ingredients and charcoals ready. Roast the first 6 ingredients until all are blackened slightly, but not burned. Cut according to suggested size. Set aside and cover.

Heat a medium casserole with butter and cooking oil. Sauté the garlic, onions, chilis, and ginger until soft. Stir in the 7 main ingredients and simmer for 5 minutes.

Add all the curry sauce ingredients-fish sauce, coconut milk, peanut butter and spices. Simmer for 20 minutes.

Put the curried stew in a serving bowl. Serve immediately.

Serving suggestion:

You may drizzle with your favorite sour cream sauce or Greek yoghurt. Serve with sticky rice or sour dough bread with fresh guacamole salad.

Fried Fish with Thai Sate' Sauce

Busy chefs can easily cook this old Thai recipe with a new twist in minutes. Any fish can be used for this delicious dish.

Ingredients:

1 whole fish (salmon fillet, sea bass or St. Peter's fish)

1 cup corn or vegetable oil, for deep frying

Juice of 1 small lime

2 tbsp rock salt

½ tsp ground black peppercorns

½ tsp cayenne

½ tsp paprika

1 tbsp corn oil

1 medium chopped white onions

2 cloves chopped garlic

1 tsp chopped ginger

1 tsp chopped green chilis

3 tbsp peanut butter

1 tsp grated lime peel

2 tbsp brown sugar

For sauce:

Directions:

Rub the fish with lime juice, oil, salt and spices. Deep fry the fish, turning only once, until crisp brown. Set aside.

While frying, heat small saucepan with cooking oil to sauté the garlic, onions, chilis, and ginger until soft. Stir in sauce ingredients and simmer for 5 minutes until it thickens.

Transfer the fried fish on a fish platter. Pour over the sate' peanut sauce and serve immediately.

Serving suggestion:

Serve with fresh cucumber slices or pesto risotto with milk shake.

Baked Fish in Spiced Potato

Even young teens can easily cook this recipe in minutes. Any fish and root vegetables can be used for this delicious dish.

Ingredients:

1 whole fish (salmon fillet, cod or red snapper)

1 cup corn or vegetable oil, for deep frying

Juice of 1 small lemon

1 tsp rock salt

1 tsp fish sauce

¼ tsp ground black peppercorns

¼ tsp ground cumin

1 tsp chopped coriander

For potato bed:

5 cups potatoes, boiled and mashed

1 tsp salt

1 liter water

1 tbsp coconut or vegetable oil

1 butter stick, softened

3 cloves garlic, finely chopped

2 pcs chopped fresh sage leaves

2 pcs chopped fresh basil leaves

¼ tsp paprika

¼ tsp cayenne

Directions:

Pre-heat the oven at 350°. Rub the fish with lemon juice, oil, fish sauce, salt and spices. Deep fry the fish, turning only once, until crisp brown. Set aside.

While frying, heat a pot with water, salt and oil to cook the potatoes for 15-20 minutes. Peel and mash the potatoes. Mix in the garlic, butter, herbs and spices.

Transfer the mashed potatoes on a baking dish and put on the top the fried fish. Put inside the pre-heated oven and bake for 10 minutes.

Put a dash of paprika and serve immediately.

Serving suggestion:

Serve with fresh cucumber slices and rice noodles.

Baked Whole Chicken with Spiced Fillings

Dads and kids will surely love this Thai dish with some twist from the West. Healthy and budget-friendly, you may add in leftovers and day-old bread for the stuffing.

Ingredients:

For the baked chicken:

1 whole chicken (or turkey)

1/2 cup olive or vegetable oil, for brushing the chicken

Juice of 1 small lemon

Juice of 1 small lime

1 tsp rock salt

½ cup fish sauce

½ cup soy sauce

¼ tsp ground black pepper

¼ tsp ground cumin

2 pcs chopped fresh basil leaves

2 pcs chopped fresh chives

1 tsp chopped parsley

For stuffing:

½ cup sweet potatoes, boiled and mashed

½ cup pineapple tidbits, chopped

½ cup red apples, chopped

½ cup green peas

¼ cup chopped anchovies

¼ cup leftovers

¼ cup day old bread

2 tbsp sesame oil

1 butter stick, softened

3 cloves garlic, finely chopped

2 pcs chopped fresh dill leaves

2 pcs chopped fresh basil leaves

1 tsp chopped green chilis, seeded

¼ tsp paprika

Directions:

Pre-heat the oven at 350°. Rub the chicken (or turkey) with lemon and lime juice, oil, fish sauce, salt, herbs and spices. Marinate at least 1 hour before baking.

While marinating, prepare the stuffing ingredients. Peel and mash the sweet potatoes. Set aside and cover.

Heat the saucepan and sauté the garlic, herbs and spices with butter. Add in all the vegetables, fruits and stuffing ingredients. Mix and sauté for 5 minutes set aside and cool slightly.

Stuff the chicken with the filling ingredients. Cover with banana leaves or aluminum foil. Place in a baking dish. Put inside the pre-heated oven and bake for 30-45 minutes.

Put a dash of paprika and honey, serve immediately.

Serving suggestion:
Serve with steamed rice or boiled rice noodles.

Stir-fried Seafood with Spiced Vegetables

Young kids can easily cook this healthy and budget-friendly dish.

Ingredients:

2 cups fresh clams, washed and drained

2 cups fresh mussels, washed and drained

2 pcs fresh big squids, washed and cut into rings

2 pcs fresh crabs, washed and halved

1 cup fresh prawns, washed and shelled

2 cups green string beans, cut into 3" long

2 cups squash, cubes 2"

3 tbsp sesame oil

1 medium white onions, sliced

3 tbsp tamarind juice

Juice of 1 small lime

½ tsp rock salt

¼ cup fish sauce

¼ cup soy sauce

2 tbsp shrimp paste

2 cups coconut milk

1 tsp ground white peppercorns

¼ tsp ground cumin

¼ tsp turmeric powder

2 pcs chopped fresh chives

1 tsp chopped parsley

Directions:

Heat the pan and sauté the onions with sesame oil. Stir-fry in all the seafood and squash. Mix the ingredients, cover and cook for 5 minutes.

Add in all the other remaining ingredients and cook for 10 minutes more.

Transfer the stir-fried dish to a serving platter. Serve immediately.

Serving suggestion:

Serve with Java rice or fresh arugula and tomato salad with Sake or white wine.

Baked Lamb Leg with Aubergines and Sweet-spicy Stuffing

Just roll up the meat and bake, you'll enjoy this delicious lamb leg.

Ingredients:

1 pc lamb leg, deboned

1 large aubergine, round slices

3 tbsp sesame oil

¼ tsp paprika

2 pcs chopped fresh basil leaves

1 tsp cloves

a dash of salt and pepper

3 tbsp tamarind juice

3 tbsp brown sugar

½ cup fresh coconut milk

¼ cup chopped anchovies

2 tbsp sesame oil

1 butter stick, softened

3 cloves garlic, finely chopped

2 pcs chopped fresh mint leaves

1 tsp chopped green chilis, seeded

¼ tsp paprika ¼ tsp nutmeg

¼ tsp cinnamon

For stuffing:

½ cup fresh prawns, shelled and chopped

½ cup squash, peeled and mashed

½ cup red apples, chopped

Sauce:

¼ cup fish sauce

¼ cup soy sauce

½ cup fresh coconut milk

1 pc chopped finger green chilis

1 tsp fresh tamarind juice

1 tsp brown sugar

Directions:

Pre-heat the oven at 400°. Cover the lamb leg with seasonings. Pan-fry the aubergines and lamb meat, set aside.

Heat the pan and sauté the garlic with sesame oil. Add in all the stuffing ingredients, cover and cook for 5 minutes. Cool slightly.

Stuff the fillings into the lamb of leg and put the aubergine slices on top. Roll up the meat and tie with strings. Transfer to a baking dish. Pour the coconut milk and sugar. Bake it for 30 minutes or until meat is tender.

In a sauce bowl, combine and stir the sauce ingredients.

Transfer the baked lamb to a serving platter. Serve immediately with prepared fish sauce.

Serving suggestion:

Serve with potato salad or fresh lettuce and tomato salad with red wine.

Spice and Sour Thai Seafood and Chicken Stew

This delicious recipe is packed with vitamins and goes well with your favorite rice or noodles.

Ingredients:

2 cups chicken, deboned and cubed 1"

1 cup salmon, deboned and cubed 1"

1 cup tuna, deboned and cubed 1"

2 cups lobster claws

2 cups prawns, shelled

2 cups mussels, washed and drained

1 large aubergine, cut lengthwise

3 tbsp sesame oil

1 pc red bell peppers, minced

1 tsp paprika

¼ tsp ground cumin

2 pcs chopped fresh basil leaves

a dash of salt and pepper

5 tbsp tamarind juice

Juice of 1 small lime

3 tbsp brown sugar

2 cups fresh coconut milk

Directions:

Heat the casserole and sauté the red bell peppers with sesame oil until soft. Add in all the chicken and seafood, and simmer for 5 minutes.

Add in and stir all the remaining ingredients. Cover and simmer for 10 minutes.

Transfer the stew to a big bowl. Serve immediately.

Serving suggestion:

Serve with fresh cucumber, green mango or turnip slices and steamed rice.

Stir-fried Rice and Egg Noodles with Chinese Cabbage

This delicious stir-fry is packed with vitamins and goes well with your favorite rice or bread.

Ingredients:

1 cup chicken, deboned and sliced thinly

½ cup pork, sliced thinly

½ cup pork liver, sliced thinly

2 cups rice noodles, soaked in cold water

2 cups egg noodles

1 cup Shiitake mushrooms, sliced thinly

1 cup Chinese cabbage, sliced thinly

1 cup snow peas, ends trimmed

3 tbsp sesame oil

3 cloves garlic, sliced thinly

½ cup celery stick, minced

1 pc red bell peppers, sliced thinly

¼ tsp paprika

¼ tsp cayenne

a dash of salt and pepper

5 tbsp tamarind juice

3 tbsp brown sugar

2 cups chicken stock

1 cup light soy sauce

Toppings:

2 eggs, scrambled and sliced thinly

1 tbsp toasted sesame seeds

Directions:

Marinate the chicken, liver and pork with tamarind sauce. Set aside.

Heat the casserole and sauté the red bell peppers, garlic and celery with sesame oil until soft. Add in all the chicken, pork and liver, and stir-fry for 5 minutes. Mix in the vegetables, noodles and stir-fry with the remaining ingredients. Cover and cook for additional 5 minutes.

Transfer the noodles to a big platter. Top with eggs and toasted sesame seeds. Serve immediately.

Serving suggestion:

Serve with steamed rice or your favorite soft bread and orange juice.

Stir-fried Rice Noodles with Oriental Veggies

This delicious stir-fried rice noodles is packed with vitamins and protein that keeps the kids energize all day long.

Ingredients:

1 cup prawns, shelled

½ cup chicken gizzard, sliced thinly

½ cup pork liver, sliced thinly

3 cups rice noodles, soaked in cold water

1 cup oyster mushrooms, sliced thinly

1 cup pechay, sliced thinly

1 cup green string beans, ends trimmed and sliced 3"

½ cup leeks, sliced thinly

3 tbsp sesame oil

3 cloves garlic, sliced thinly

½ cup white onions, minced

1 tsp fresh ground black pepper

¼ tsp cayenne

5 tbsp tamarind juice

2 pcs chopped red chilis

3 tbsp brown sugar

2 cups chicken stock

1 cup light soy sauce

2 tbsp fish sauce

Toppings:

2 eggs, scrambled and sliced thinly

1 tbsp toasted sesame seeds

1 tbsp chopped fresh cilantro leaves

Directions:

Marinate the prawns, liver and gizzard with tamarind sauce and chilis. Set aside.

Heat the casserole and sauté the garlic and onions with sesame oil until soft. Add in all the prawns, gizzards and liver, and stir-fry for 5 minutes. Mix in the vegetables, noodles and stir-fry with the remaining ingredients. Cover and cook for additional 5-8 minutes.

Transfer the noodles to a big platter. Top with eggs, cilantro and toasted sesame seeds. Serve immediately.

Serving suggestion:

Serve with your favorite soup and juice.

Egg Noodle Soup with Stewed Vegetables and Fish

This is packed with vitamins and protein that keeps the kids warm all night long. Its oriental flavor is impressive and can be cooked anytime of the week.

Ingredients:

3 cups egg noodles

3 tbsp sesame oil

5 cups chicken stock

½ cup light soy sauce

½ cup sweet potatoes, cubed 1"

½ cup tomatoes, cubed 1"

½ cup leeks, sliced thinly

1 tsp fresh ground black pepper

¼ tsp cayenne

5 tbsp tamarind juice

2 pcs chopped red chilis

2 cups coconut milk

2 tbsp fish sauce

Stew mixture:

1 cup salmon, deboned and cubed 1"

½ cup tuna, deboned and cubed 1"

½ cup button mushrooms, sliced thinly

Directions:

Put the chicken stock in a pot and let it boil. Add in all the noodles, sesame oil and soy sauce. Boil for 3 minutes. Set aside uncovered so as not to overcook.

In a separate pot, boil the coconut and tamarind sauce. Add in all the stew ingredients and let it boil for 5 minutes and stir once. Mix in the noodle mixture and cook further for 5 minutes.

Transfer the noodle soup to a serving bowl. You may top with toasted garlic and chives. Serve immediately.

Serving suggestion:

Serve with your favorite bread or fried tofu slices.

Braised Pork with Anise Sauce

Braised pork taste deliciously with any spices, like anise and nutmeg, combined with vegetables and seasonings. This old recipe with a new twist is easy to prepare and cook.

Ingredients:

3 cups pork tenderloin, cubed 2"

1 cup pork ribs, sliced lengthwise

1 cup pork cubes with fat, cubed 2"

3 tbsp sesame oil

5 cups stock

1 cup thick coconut milk

½ cup light soy sauce

½ cup potatoes, cubed 1"

½ tsp fresh ground black pepper

a pinch of cumin

1 tsp cloves

½ cup tamarind juice

2 pcs chopped red chilis

½ cup cold water

2 tbsp cornstarch

2 tbsp fish sauce

Anise sauce:

1 cup anise, boiled with water

1 cup Portobello mushrooms, sliced thinly

½ cup garbanzos, boiled and drained

Toppings: (toast together)

1 tsp toasted sesame seeds

1 tbsp toasted peanuts

Directions:

Put the stock in a pot and let it boil. Add in all the pork and let it boil for 5 minutes. Add and stir in the sesame oil, coconut milk and soy sauce. Boil for 30 minutes or until meat is tender.

While cooking the meat, in a separate pot, boil the anise seeds and water for 10 minutes. Strain the boiled water using a cheesecloth or strainer.

In the same pot, boil the anise water together with the rest of the sauce ingredients for 5 minutes and stir until sauce thickens.

Place the cooked meat in a serving bowl and pour the anise sauce. Top with toasted sesame seeds and peanuts. Serve immediately.

Serving suggestion:

Serve with garlic rice or steamed buns.

Boiled Beef Brisket with Thai's Veggies

Boiled beef taste deliciously with any vegetables and seasonings. This old recipe is packed with vitamins and carbohydrates.

Ingredients:

3 cups beef brisket, cubed 2"

1 cup beef chuck, cubed 2"

1 cup beef ribs, sliced lengthwise

1 cup beef flanks with fat, cubed 2"

3 tbsp sesame oil

7 cups water

1 cup thick coconut milk

1 pc green chilli finger, halved

1 pc white onion, quartered

1 tsp cloves

1 pc cinnamon stick

½ cup light soy sauce

Veggie mixture:

1 cup carrots, julienned

3 pcs shiitake mushrooms, sliced thinly

½ cup potatoes, cubed 1"

3 pcs yellow corn on a cob, cut into 3s

½ tsp fresh ground black pepper

a pinch of cumin

½ cup lime juice

2 pcs chopped red chilis

2 pcs chopped fresh bay leaves

2 pcs chopped fresh dill leaves

½ cup cold water

3 tbsp cornstarch

2 tbsp fish sauce

3 tbsp sesame oil

Directions:

Put the stock in a pot and let it boil. Add in all the beef and let it boil for 5 minutes. Add and stir in the sesame oil, coconut milk, soy sauce and all the main ingredients. Boil for 30 minutes or until meat is tender.

In a separate casserole, heat the sesame oil. Add in all the vegetables and stir-fry for 3 minutes.

Then combined all the veggie mixture, simmer for 10 more minutes.

Place the cooked beef in a serving bowl and pour the veggie mixture. Serve immediately.

Serving suggestion:

Serve with mashed potato salad or sour dough bread.

Chicken ala Kai Phat Khing

Kai Phat Khing is a delicious stir-fried chicken in Central Thailand. This recipe is budgetfriendly and quick to cook.

Ingredients:

2 cups chicken breast fillets, sliced thinly

1 tbsp fresh ginger root, sliced thinly

3 tbsp sesame oil

½ cup coconut milk

½ cup chicken stock

2 tbsp soy sauce

Thick sauce:

1 pc green chilli finger, chopped

1 pc chopped red chilis

2 pcs chopped fresh bay leaves

1 pc white onion, chopped

½ cup light soy sauce

½ tsp fresh ground black pepper

½ cup lime juice

½ cup cold water

3 tbsp cornstarch

2 tbsp fish sauce

3 tbsp sesame oil

Directions:

In saucepan heat the sesame oil with ginger and stir-fry the chicken until it turns white and no visible blood. Add in the stock and soy sauce. Cover and simmer for 5 minutes.

In a separate saucepan, heat the sesame oil. Add in the entire ingredient and stir-fry for 3 minutes. Transfer to a blender or food processor, puree it for 5 seconds. OR pound the ingredients in a mortar and pestle.

Add the puree and pour with the stir-fried chicken. Cook the stir-fry dish for additional 5 minutes or until sauce thickens.

Transfer in flat platter. Serve immediately.

Serving suggestion:

Serve with steamed broccoli and cauliflower florets and fresh mango shakes.

Rice Noodles ala Khanom chin nam ngiao

Khanom chin nam ngiao is a delicious delicacy in Northern Thailand. This recipe is unique and easy to cook. You may omit the pork blood and use tofu instead.

Ingredients:

3 cups Thai fermented rice noodles

1 cup pork meat, sliced thinly

1 cup pork blood, steamed and cut into squares

1 cup tofu squares, quartered and deep fried

1 tbsp fresh onions, sliced thinly

3 tbsp sesame oil

1 cup stock

2 tbsp soy sauce

Thick sauce:

2 cups red tomatoes, diced

1 pc chopped red chilis, fried

½ cup fermented soy beans (tausi beans)

1 cup bamboo shoots, sliced thinly

1 cup coconut milk

1 tsp lime juice

1 tsp tamarind juice

Directions:

In saucepan heat the sesame oil and stir-fry the pork blood squares until it turns soft. Add in the stock, seasoning and soy sauce. Cover and simmer for 5 minutes. Add the rice noodles and boil for 5 minutes.

In a separate saucepan, heat the coconut milk and let it boil with lime and tamarind sauce. Stir it constantly so it will not curdle. Add in the entire sauce ingredients and simmer for 5 minutes.

Transfer in a big bowl the cooked noodles and pour the cooked sauce. Serve immediately.

Serving suggestion:

Serve with almond bread and fresh cantaloupe smoothie.

Rice Soup ala Khanom chin nam ngiao

Khanom chin nam ngiao is a delicious delicacy in Northern Thailand. This recipe is unique and easy to cook. You may omit the pork blood and use tofu instead.

Ingredients:

2 cups long grain rice, washed and drained

1 cup pork meat, sliced thinly

1 cup pork blood, steamed and cut into squares

1 cup tofu squares, quartered and deep fried

1 tbsp fresh chives, sliced thinly

1 tbsp fresh leeks, sliced thinly

1 tbsp fresh shallots, sliced thinly

3 tbsp sesame oil

5-7 cups stock or water

2 tbsp fish sauce

Flavourings and vegetables:

1 cup red beefsteak tomatoes, quartered

1 cup green unripe cherry tomatoes, whole

1 pc chopped red chilis, fried

½ cup fermented soy beans (tausi beans)

½ cup bamboo shoots, sliced thinly

½ cup carrots, sliced thinly

1 cup coconut milk

1 tsp lime juice

1 tsp tamarind juice

a dash of paprika

a pinch of salt and pepper

Directions:

In saucepan heat the sesame oil and stir-fry the pork blood squares until it turns soft. Add in the stock, rice, seasoning and fish sauce. Cover and simmer for 5 minutes. Add the rice grain and boil for 15 minutes.

In a separate saucepan, heat the coconut milk and let it boil with lime and tamarind sauce. Stir it constantly so it will not curdle.

Add in the entire flavoring and vegetable ingredients and simmer for 5 minutes.

Transfer in a big bowl the cooked rice soup and pour the vegetable mixture. Serve immediately.

Serving suggestion:

Serve with wheat bread and fresh winter melon smoothie.

Glutinous Rice Soup ala Khao Man Kai

Khao man kai is delicious steamed rice from Northern Thailand. This recipe will surely be liked by kids.

Ingredients:

2 cups long grain glutinous rice, washed and drained

1 cup chicken, sliced in cubes 2"

3 cloves garlic, sliced thinly

1 tbsp fresh shallots, sliced thinly

3 tbsp corn oil

5-7 cups chicken stock

Flavourings:

3 tbsp fish sauce

a dash of paprika

a pinch of salt and pepper

Directions:

In a saucepan heat the corn oil, garlic, shallots and stir-fry the chicken cubes until it turns soft. Add in the stock, seasoning and fish sauce. Cover and simmer for 5 minutes. Add the rice grain and boil for 15 minutes.

Transfer in a big bowl the cooked rice soup and put a dash of paprika, salt and pepper. Serve immediately.

Serving suggestion:

Serve with pita bread or tortilla wraps and fresh water melon smoothie.

Spicy Shrimp and Red Rice ala Khao Man Kai

Khao man kai is delicious steamed rice from Northern Thailand. This recipe is added with a western twist to easily prepare and cook in time.

Ingredients:

2 cups long grain red rice, washed and drained

1 cup shrimps, shelled and deveined

1 cup chicken breast fillets, sliced thinly

7 cups chicken stock

3 cloves garlic, sliced thinly

2 tbsp fresh shallots, sliced thinly

3 tbsp corn oil

Flavourings and vegetable mixture:

3 tbsp fish sauce

1 tsp cayenne

1 tsp chopped red chilis

3 pcs Portobello mushrooms, sliced thinly

½ cup zucchini, minced

a dash of paprika

a pinch of salt and pepper

Directions:

In a saucepan heat the corn oil, garlic, shallots and stir-fry the chicken cubes until it turns soft. Add in the stock, seasoning and fish sauce. Cover and simmer for 5 minutes. Add the rice grain and boil for 15 minutes.

Mix in the flavourings, herbs and vegetable mixture with additional cup of stock to keep rice soupy and not dry.

Transfer in a big bowl the cooked rice soup and put a dash of paprika, salt and pepper. Serve immediately.

Serving suggestion:

Serve with tortilla wraps, fried pork chops and fresh mango smoothie.

Sweet and Sour Rice ala Khao Phat

Khao phat is an appetizing rice favorite from Northern Thailand. This recipe is added with some vegetables and ingredients readily available in your pantry.

Ingredients:

3 cups white rice, washed and drained

1 cup shrimps, shelled and deveined

½ cup crab meat, shelled and flaked

1 cup chicken breast fillets, sliced thinly

½ cup beef strips, sliced thinly

½c up pork liver sliced thinly

½ cup pineapple tidbits

½ cup carrots, grated

½ cup coconut meat, sliced

¼ cup raisins

5 cups chicken stock

3 cloves garlic, sliced thinly

2 tbsp fresh shallots, sliced thinly

3 tbsp corn oil

Flavourings:

5 tbsp fish sauce

1 tbsp shrimp paste

3 tbsp lemon juice

3 tbsp brown sugar

1 tsp chopped green chilis

½ tsp cayenne

a dash of paprika

a pinch of salt and pepper

Directions:

In a saucepan heat the corn oil, garlic, shallots and stir-fry the meat until it turns soft. Add in the stock, seasoning and fish sauce. Cover and simmer for 5 minutes. Add the rice grain and boil for 15 minutes.

Mix in the flavourings, sugar, herbs and spices with additional cup of stock to keep rice sticky and not dry.

Transfer in a big bowl the cooked rice and put a dash of paprika, salt and pepper. Serve immediately with lemon wedges.

Serving suggestion:

Serve with tortilla wraps, fried chicken drumsticks and fresh carrot smoothie.

Khao Phat ala Paella Rice

Paella is a sumptuous dish. Khao phat is an appetizing rice favorite from Northern Thailand. This recipe is added with some vegetables and ingredients readily available in your pantry.

Ingredients:

3 cups glutinous rice, washed and drained

1 cup mussels, washed and drained

1 cup prawns, shelled and deveined

½ cup lobster meat, shelled and flaked

1 cup chicken breast fillets, sliced thinly

½ cup beef strips, sliced thinly

½c up pork liver, sliced thinly

½ cup pineapple tidbits

½ cup carrots, grated

¼ cup frozen green peas

¼ cup raisins

5 cups chicken stock

3 cloves garlic, sliced thinly

2 tbsp fresh shallots, sliced thinly

5 tbsp annatto oil

Flavourings:

5 tbsp fish sauce

1 tbsp shrimp paste

1 tsp chopped green chilis

¼ tsp cumin powder

a dash of garlic salt

a pinch of salt and pepper

1 tbsp chopped cilantro

Toppings:

3 large eggs, boiled, shelled and halved

½ cup pork cracklings, crushed

3-5 lemon wedges

Directions:

In a saucepan heat the annatto oil, garlic, shallots and stir-fry the meat and seafood until it turns soft. Add in the stock, ingredients, seasoning and fish sauce. Cover and simmer for 5 minutes. Add in the rice grain and boil for 15 minutes.

Mix in the flavourings, herbs and spices with additional cup of stock to keep rice sticky and not dry. Cover with banana leaves (or aluminum foil) and cook further for 5 minutes

Transfer in a big platter the cooked rice and arranged the toppings around. Put a dash of salt and pepper. Serve immediately.

Serving suggestion:

Serve with wheat tortilla wraps, braised pork and fresh banana smoothie.

Boiled Pork Hamloin ala Khao Phat

Boiled pork hamloin is a sumptuous treat rich in vitamins and yumminess. This Khao phat recipe is an appetizing rice favorite of Thais, I added with some vegetables and ingredients readily available in your pantry for easier cooking.

Ingredients:

1 whole pork ham loin, deboned and boiled

5 cups stock + 2 cups water, for pork

1 cup glutinous rice, washed and drained

1 cup red ripe apples, finely chopped

½ cup frozen green peas

¼ cup raisins, finely chopped

½ cup chicken breast fillets, finely chopped

5 cups stock, for rice

3 cloves garlic, sliced thinly

2 tbsp fresh shallots, sliced thinly

1 tsp dried cloves

5 tbsp annatto oil

Flavourings and sauce:

5 tbsp cornstarch

1 cup cold water

1 cup sour cream

5 tbsp fish sauce

1 tsp chopped green chilis

¼ tsp cumin powder

a dash of garlic salt

a pinch of salt and pepper

1 tbsp chopped chives

1 tbsp chopped parsley

Directions:

In a big pot fill it with water and stock. Boil the stock with deboned pork hamloin until soft and tender.

In a saucepan heat the annatto oil, garlic, shallots and stir-fry the chicken and apples until it turns soft. Add in the stock, ingredients, seasoning and fish sauce. Cover and simmer for 5 minutes. Add in the rice grain and boil for 15 minutes.

Mix in the flavourings, sauce, herbs and spices with additional cup of stock to keep rice sticky and not dry. Cover with banana leaves (or aluminum foil) and cook further for 5 minutes.

Transfer in a big platter the cooked rice. Cut the boiled pork hamloin and arranged into the top of cooked rice. Serve immediately.

Serving suggestion:

Serve with pita bread or greens salad and fresh banana smoothie.

Khanom chin namya Rice Noodles

Khanom chin namya is a sumptuous treat rich in vitamins and protein. An appetizing rice noodles favorite of Thais with basic ingredients.

Ingredients:

3 cups rice noodles

2 cups stock + 1 cup water, for noodles

2 tbsp annatto oil

1 cup Chinese cabbage, shredded

1 cup Kangkong leaves (water spinach), washed and drained

3 cloves garlic, chopped

Flavourings and sauce:

½ cup fish sauce

½ cup oyster sauce

½ cup stock

5 tbsp cornstarch

1 cup cold water

1 tsp chopped green chilis

a pinch of salt and pepper

1 tbsp chopped chives

Directions:

In a big pot fill it with water and stock. Boil the stock with deboned rice noodles for 5-8 minutes.

In a saucepan heat the annatto oil, garlic and stir-fry the leafy vegetables until it turns soft. Set aside.

In a small pot, bring to a boil the stock. Mix in the slurry (mixed cornstarch and cold water), seasonings, spices, and oyster and fish sauce. Cover and simmer for 5 minutes.

Transfer the cooked rice noodles in a big platter. Arrange the vegetables around the noodles. Pour the sauce and serve immediately.

Serving suggestion:

Serve with roti bread or greens salad and fresh strawberry smoothie.

Egg and Vermicelli Noodles
ala Khanom chin namya

Khanom chin namya is a mouth-watering noodle treat rich in carbohydrates and protein to last you all day long. An appetizing rice noodles favorite of Thais with basic ingredients such as fish sauce.

Ingredients:

2 cups egg noodles

2 cups Vermicelli noodles, soaked in water

3 cups stock + 1 cup water, for noodles

2 cups chicken, cubed 2"

2 tbsp corn oil

1 cup carrots, shredded

1 cup green wax beans, cut into 2"

1 cup Kangkong leaves (water spinach), washed and drained

½ cup onions, chopped

3 cloves garlic, chopped

Flavourings and sauce:

½ cup fish sauce

½ cup oyster sauce

½ cup brown sugar

1 cup stock

5 tbsp cornstarch

1 cup cold water

1 tsp chopped red chilis

a pinch of salt and pepper

1 tbsp chopped chives

1 tsp toasted sesame seeds

1 tsp toasted chopped nuts

Directions:

In a big pot fill it with water and stock. Boil the stock with rice and egg noodles for 5-8 minutes.

In a saucepan heat the corn oil, garlic, onions and stir-fry the leafy chicken until it turns soft. Add in the vegetable and stir-fry for 3 minutes. Set aside.

In a small pot, bring to a boil the stock. Mix in the slurry (mixed cornstarch and cold water), seasonings, spices, and oyster and fish sauce. Cover and simmer for 5 minutes.

Transfer the cooked rice noodles in a big platter. Arrange the vegetables around the noodles. Pour the sauce and serve immediately.

Serving suggestion:

Serve with French bread or greens salad and fresh avocado smoothie.

Lemon Pork and Dory Fish Fillets with Thai Sauce

This is A+ rich and delicious pork and fish fillets with the zest of lemon and Thai sauce.

Ingredients:

1 cup all-purpose flour

3 eggs, whisked

2 cups pork, cubed 2"

2 cups dory fish fillets, cubed 2"

1 pc of lemon, squeezed for juice and grated peel

1 cup corn oil

a dash of salt and pepper to taste

a dash of paprika

a pinch of cumin

Flavourings and sauce:

½ cup fish sauce

½ cup oyster sauce

½ cup brown sugar

1 cup stock

5 tbsp cornstarch

1 cup cold water

1 tsp chopped red chilli

Directions:

Whisk the egg in a bowl and add a dash of salt and pepper, lemon juice and grated peel. Soak all the meat and fish in the egg mixture for atleast an hour. Cover and set aside in the fridge.

Prepare the flour in a flat dish or tray. Mix with cumin and paprika. Dredge the pork and fish with flour. Set aside.

In a big frying pan fill it with corn oil and put in high heat. Deep-fry the pork and fish for 5-8 minutes until golden brown. Drain and set aside.

In a small pot, bring to a boil the stock. Mix in the slurry (mixed cornstarch and cold water), seasonings, spices, and oyster and fish sauce. Cover and simmer for 5 minutes until sauce thickens.

Transfer the fried pork and fish in a big platter. Pour the sauce and serve immediately.

Serving suggestion:

You may top the pork and fish fillets with sesame seeds and roasted nuts. Serve with steamed rice or greens salad and fresh melon smoothie.

Beef Strips and Onion Rings with Thai Sauce

This is a rich and delicious beef and onion rings with the zest of lemon and Thai sauce.

Ingredients:

1 cup all-purpose flour

3 eggs, whisked

2 cups beef strips

2 cups onion rings

1 tbsp lemon juice

1 tsp grated lemon peel

1 cup corn oil

a dash of salt and pepper to taste

a dash of paprika

a pinch of turmeric powder

Flavourings and sauce:

5 tbsp fish sauce

½ cup peanut butter

½ cup brown sugar

1 cup stock

5 tbsp cornstarch

1 cup cold water

1 tsp chopped red chilli

1 tbsp chopped red onions

1 tsp toasted sesame seeds

1 tsp toasted chopped peanuts

Directions:

Whisk the egg in a bowl and add a dash of salt and pepper, lemon juice and grated peel. Soak all the beef and onion rings in the egg mixture for atleast an hour. Cover and set aside in the fridge.

Prepare the flour in a flat dish or tray. Mix with turmeric powder and paprika. Dredge the beef and onion rings with flour. Set aside.

In a big frying pan fill it with corn oil and put in high heat. Deep-fry the beef and onion rings for 5 minutes until golden brown. Drain and set aside.

In a small pot, bring to a boil the stock. Mix in the slurry (mixed cornstarch and cold water), peanut butter, seasonings, spices, fish sauce. Cover and simmer for 5 minutes until sauce thickens.

Transfer the deep-fried beef strips and onion rings in a big platter. Pour the sauce and serve immediately.

Serving suggestion:

You may top the dish with sesame seeds and roasted nuts. Serve with garlic rice or pesto pasta and fresh melon smoothie.

Beef Rolls with Thai Sauce

This is a rich and delicious beef and onion rings with the zest of lemon and Thai sauce.

Ingredients:

6-8 pcs beef flanks, cut into thin, flat wide strips

1 tbsp lemon juice

½ cup corn oil

a dash of salt and pepper to taste

a dash of paprika

a pinch of cayenne

a pinch of cumin

Stuffing:

1 pc grated carrots

½ cup chopped raisins

1 cup cucumbers, seeded and julienned

½ cup chopped peanuts

½ cup desiccated coconut

Flavourings and sauce:

5 tbsp soy sauce

5 tbsp oyster sauce

½ cup peanut butter

½ cup brown sugar

1 cup stock

1 tsp chopped red chilli

1 tsp tamarind sauce

Directions:

Marinate the beef with lemon juice and seasonings. Pan-fry the beef wraps for a minute. Then lay flat on a clean tray or plate.

Mix the stuffing in a clean bowl. Place 2 tablespoons of stuffing on the beef wraps and roll up. Set aside on a serving platter.

In a saucepan fill it with sauce ingredients in high heat. Simmer for 5 minutes until sauce thickens. Pour over the beef wraps and serve immediately.

Serving suggestion:

Serve with pesto rice and hot cocoa drink.

Cabbage Rolls with Veggie-Nut and Thai Sauce

This is a rich and cabbage rolls with the veggie-nut concoction and Thai sauce.

Ingredients:

8-10 pcs cabbage leaves, boiled and cut into thin, flat wide wraps (remove hard core)
1 cup stock
1 tbsp lemon juice
a dash of salt and pepper to taste

Stuffing:

5 pcs baby asparagus, halved ½ cup chopped raisins
½ cup zucchinis, julienned
½ cup chopped peanuts
½ cup chopped roasted chestnuts
½ cup desiccated coconut

a dash of paprika
a pinch of cayenne
a pinch of cumin
a dash of salt and pepper to taste

Flavourings and sauce:

1 cup stock
5 tbsp soy sauce
5 tbsp oyster sauce
5 tbsp brown sugar
½ cup peanut butter
1 tsp chopped red chilli

Directions:

Boil a pot with stock and lemon juice. Put the cabbage and a dash of salt and pepper. Boil it for 5 minutes or until soft. Drain. Then lay flat on a clean tray or plate.

Mix the stuffing in a clean bowl. Place 2 tablespoons of stuffing on the cabbage wraps and roll up. Tie with chives or secure with toothpicks. Set aside on a serving platter.

In a saucepan fill it with sauce ingredients in high heat. Simmer for 5 minutes until sauce thickens. Pour over the cabbage wraps and serve immediately. (*remove the toothpicks before serving)

Serving suggestion:

Serve with pesto pasta and red wine.

Chicken & Bok Choy Soup
with Ginger & Mushrooms

Absolutely delicious & tempting! I have made it a couple of times & added Fresno pepper slices.

To make it a bit tangy, feel free to serve it with lemon wedges on a side and enjoy.

Ingredients

2 pounds skinless, boneless chicken thighs, trimmed & cut into 1" pieces

1 bulb fennel, cored & cut into 1" pieces

½ oz. mixed dried or dried shiitake mushrooms

2 cups mung bean sprouts (approximately 4 oz.)

1 whole star anise

2 cups onion, diced

1 tablespoon canola oil or peanut oil

3 garlic cloves, thinly sliced

1 cinnamon stick (2 to 3")

6 slices of fresh ginger (each 1/8" thick), peeled

¼ cup soy sauce, low-sodium

6 cups chicken broth, low-sodium

1 teaspoon freshly ground pepper

8 scallions, whites cut into 2" pieces & greens chopped, divided

1 pound baby bok choy, white stems sliced lengthwise & greens chopped, divided

2 teaspoons toasted sesame oil

½ cup fresh cilantro, chopped

3 cups boiling water

Directions

Cover the mushrooms with boiling water in a heatproof measuring cup. Let soak for half an hour. Remove the mushrooms & discard the stems, cut into 1/8" slices & set aside. Strain & set the soaking liquid aside.

Next, over moderate heat in a Dutch oven or large soup pot, heat up the oil until hot. Add onion, ginger and garlic, cook for 5 minutes, stirring frequently. Pour in the kept-aside mushroom liquid followed by soy sauce, star anise, cinnamon stick, broth & pepper, bring the mix to a boil, over moderate heat. Decrease the heat and let simmer. Once done, immediately stir in the chicken & let simmer for 17 to 20 minutes.

Stir in the fennel, the reserved mushrooms and scallion whites, cook for a couple of minutes. Add the bok choy stems, bring it to a simmer again & cook for 3 more minutes. Stir in the bean sprouts and bok choy greens. Cook for 2 more minutes, until the greens are just wilted.

Discard the star anise and cinnamon stick. Ladle the soup into individual bowls. Garnish each bowl with the cilantro, scallion greens and a ¼ teaspoon drizzle of the sesame oil. Serve hot and enjoy.

Asian Chicken Noodle Soup

I often try this recipe for my guests. It takes very less time and effort to prepare it. All of my guests just love the taste and ask for more.

Ingredients

2 tablespoons vegetable oil

1 cup carrots (approximately 2 large), diced

2 tablespoons ginger, peeled & minced

1 ½ cups green onions, sliced (approximately 6)

3 cups slightly packed chopped Napa cabbage

4 garlic cloves, minced

1 pound skinless, boneless chicken breasts

6 ½ cups chicken broth, low-sodium

2 ½ tablespoons soy sauce, or to taste

1 tablespoon granulated sugar

2 tablespoons mirin

1 tablespoon Sriracha

2 tablespoons rice vinegar

½ cup fresh cilantro, chopped

6 oz crimini mushrooms, sliced

1 tablespoon sesame oil

1 package dry ramen (4.3 oz), seasoning packets discarded

Freshly ground black or white pepper and salt to taste

Directions

Over moderate heat in a large non-stick skillet, heat up 1 tablespoon of vegetable oil until hot. Add and sauté the carrots for 3 minutes and then, add the green onions followed by ginger and garlic, continue to sauté for 2 more minutes, set the mix aside.

Using a plastic wrap, cover the chicken & pound to an even thickness using a meat mallet, preferably the flat side. Next, over moderate heat in a large pot, heat 1 tablespoon of olive oil until hot.

Lightly season the chicken with pepper and salt on both sides and then, add to the pot, cook for 2 ½ minutes on each side, until both sides turn brown.

Pour in the chicken broth followed by rice vinegar, mirin, soy sauce, sesame oil, and Sriracha, add carrot mixture into the soup mixture.

Bring the mix to a boil. Once done, decrease the heat to medium-low, cover & let simmer for 5 to 7 minutes, until the meat has cooked through.

Remove the chicken breasts from your soup & transfer to a large cutting board, let rest for a couple of minutes and then, cut into thin strips.

In the meantime, stir in sugar, mushrooms and cabbage, bring the soup to a boil again. Add the noodles & continue to cook until noodles are tender, for 3 to 5 more minutes. Stir in the chicken.

Serve warm, topped with freshly chopped cilantro and enjoy.

Chinese Noodle Soup

Absolutely delicious! The addition of oyster sauce and soy sauce gives this recipe a rich authentic taste. Feel free to add your favorite vegetables & vegetable stock. Enjoy.

Ingredients

3 green onions, sliced finely into rounds

1 tablespoon Oyster Sauce

4 oz Dried Chinese noodles

1 tablespoon dark Soy Sauce, reduced-sodium

4 leaves Bok Choy/pak choi sliced

1 tablespoon Soy Sauce, reduced-sodium

4 cups chicken stock

Directions

Over moderate heat in a large saucepan, heat up the chicken stock & bring it to a boil.

Once done, add the Chinese greens or Bok Choy followed by green onions, oyster sauce, soy sauces & noodles.

Decrease the heat & cook the noodles per the instructions until just tender, per the directions mentioned on the package.

Serve hot and enjoy.

Ginger Garlic Noodle Soup with Bok Choy

Absolutely delicious & healthy! You can prepare it easily by adding shrimp, chicken, spicy chilies, or any of your favorite veggies. Feel free to sub the chicken broth with vegetable broth and soy sauce with Tamari.

Ingredients

1 bunch green onions, chopped (white and green divided)

2 tablespoon fresh ginger, minced

4 garlic cloves, minced

1 tablespoon olive oil

3 shallots, diced

6 oz rice noodles

5 ½ cups chicken broth, low sodium

2 tablespoon soy sauce

10 oz Crimini mushrooms, sliced

1 ½ heads bok choy, chopped roughly

2 whole star anise

For Topping:

Red pepper flakes

Sesame seeds

Directions

Over moderate heat in a medium-sized stockpot, heat 2 tablespoons of olive oil until hot.

Add diced shallots to the hot oil & cook until the shallots start to soften and turn translucent, for 3 to 5 minutes, stirring frequently.

Chop the end from each green onion, remove and divide the white part from the green part. Chop & set the green part aside for later. In the meantime, finely chop the white part of every green onion.

Add white part of green onions followed by minced ginger and garlic to the shallots & continue to cook until garlic and ginger turns fragrant, for a minute or two, stirring occasionally.

Carefully pour the water or chicken stock (or a mix) into the pot & bring the mix to a simmer. Once done, add star anise & soy sauce to the pot. Cover & continue to cook for 10 minutes, over medium to low heat.

Remove the lid, carefully remove & discard star anise from your soup.

Add sliced mushrooms followed by bok choy, and uncooked noodles to the hot pot & let simmer until bok choy & noodles are tender, for 5 to 7 minutes. Season with pepper & salt to taste.

Evenly divide the soup among bowls & garnish each with the green parts of green onions, sesame seeds & red pepper flakes. Serve hot and enjoy.

Asian Broth

Absolutely delicious! Feel free to serve this delicious broth on a cold day sprinkled with a pinch or two of black pepper and enjoy the taste. You may sub the galangal with ginger as well.

Ingredients

3 stalks lemon grass, outer husk removed, cleaned & coarsely chopped

15 Kafir lime leaves, washed

2 pods large garlic, coarsely chopped

1 large piece of galangal, coarsely chopped

5 large, dry shitake mushrooms

2 star anise

1 teaspoon soy sauce

2 tablespoons brown sugar or to taste

10 cups water

2 red chilies dry, coarsely chopped

Salt to taste

Directions

Fill a large stock pot with water and all of the remaining ingredients to it.

Bring it to a boil, over moderate heat. Once done, decrease the heat to medium & let simmer until broth is decreased to half, for 20 to 25 minutes, stirring occasionally. Turn off the heat & your Asian Broth is ready.

Asian Spicy Noodle Soup

This recipe is a savior. Feel free to sub the tamari with gluten-free soy sauce and vegan broth with chicken broth. Enjoy.

Ingredients

2 teaspoons Sriracha

1 yellow onion, diced

2 garlic cloves, minced

8 oz. rice noodles

2 tablespoons organic tamari

4 cups vegetable broth

2 teaspoons fresh ginger, grated

1 teaspoon rice vinegar

2 cups water

1 tablespoon sesame oil

For Garnish, Optional:

Sliced green onions, sesame seeds, and chopped fresh cilantro

Directions

Over moderate heat in a large pot, heat up the oil until hot. Add and cook the onion until softened, for 3 to 4 minutes.

Add the ginger and garlic, sauté until fragrant, for a minute.

Add the water and broth. Increase the heat to high & bring the mix to a boil.

Once done, immediately stir in the tamari, rice vinegar and Sriracha.

Add rice noodles to the hot pot & let sit until softened, for a couple of minutes.

Just before serving, garnish your soup with the optional toppings, serve hot and enjoy.

Asian Zoodle Soup

Absolutely delicious & tempting! Feel free to serve this delicious soup with traditional Asian soup toppings and enjoy.

Ingredients

2 medium zucchini

1 medium onion, peeled

2 tablespoons canola or safflower oil, divided

1 teaspoon fresh garlic, minced

4 shiitake mushrooms, sliced thinly

½ teaspoon Chinese 5 spice powder

2 teaspoons fresh ginger, peeled & finely grated

Fresh mung bean sprouts

¼ cup soy sauce

2 lightly beaten eggs

Sriracha (chile sauce), to taste

2 tablespoons fresh cilantro, chopped

Lime wedges, fresh basil, fresh mint, fresh cilantro

1 tablespoon fresh lime juice

Reduced sodium chicken broth, as required

½ teaspoon salt

Directions

Trim the ends off of zucchini and onion and then, cut to fit spiralizer attachment, spiralize 6 cups zucchini, ½ cup onion using the fine spiralizing blade

Cut the spirals into desired lengths using a knife or kitchen shears.

Next, over moderate heat in a pot, heat up the oil until hot. Add onion, and mushroom, cook until softened & turn brown, for 5 minutes, stirring occasionally.

Add ginger followed by garlic & 5 spice powder, give the ingredients a good stir and continue to cook for half a minute more. Add soy sauce and broth, bring the mix to a simmer. Once done, decrease the heat to low and maintain the simmer. Cook for 17 to 20 minutes. Next, stir the soup and drizzle the beaten eggs into the hot soup carefully in a thin stream. Add the lime juice and cilantro.

For Zoodles: Over moderate heat in a large skillet, heat up 1 tablespoon of oil until hot. Add zoodles & sprinkle with the salt. Cook the zoodles until softened slightly & just beginning to release some of the juices, for 2 to 3 minutes, tossing frequently with the pair of tongs.

Evenly divide the zoodles among four bowls & top with the soup. Serve immediately and enjoy.

Thai Coconut Soup

The best part about this recipe is that you can enjoy it anytime during the day. Quite easy to prepare and tastes great too!

Ingredients

2 tablespoons fresh ginger, grated

½ pound fresh shiitake mushrooms, sliced

3 cans coconut milk (13.5 oz. each)

1 pound shrimp, medium-sized, peeled & deveined

2 teaspoons red curry paste

¼ cup fresh cilantro, chopped

4 cups chicken broth

1 stalk lemon grass, minced

3 tablespoons fish sauce

1 tablespoon light brown sugar

2 tablespoons lime juice, fresh

1 tablespoon vegetable oil

Salt to taste

Directions

Over moderate heat in a large pot, heat up the oil until hot. Add ginger followed by lemongrass, and curry paste, cook & stir for a minute in the hot oil.

Slowly stir in the chicken broth and then, stir in the brown sugar and fish sauce, decrease the heat to low & let simmer for 12 to 15 minutes.

Once done, add the mushrooms and coconut milk, cook & stir for 5 minutes, until mushrooms are just soft.

Add shrimp & cook for 5 more minutes, until no longer translucent. Stir in the lime juice and then, season with salt. Just before serving, garnish each serving with the cilantro.

Thai Tom Kha Soup Recipe

Absolutely delicious! You will fall in love with it. I often prepare this recipe on the weekends for my family, and they just love the taste. Feel free to sub the red pepper flakes with fresh chilies.

Ingredients

2 pounds boneless chicken thighs, cut into bite-sized pieces against the grain

¼ cup fresh cilantro, finely chopped

6 makrut lime leaves, thinly sliced

1 piece galangal (2"), thinly sliced

4 cups coconut milk

1 stalk lemongrass, tough outer parts removed, thinly sliced

2 fresh Thai chile peppers, minced

½ head cabbage, thinly sliced

Juice of 5 limes, fresh

1 cup chicken stock

¾ teaspoon fish sauce

Directions

Over high heat in a large pot, bring the chicken stock with coconut milk to a boil. Once done, decrease the heat to medium & add the lemongrass with cilantro, galangal, lime leaves, and Thai chile peppers, let simmer for a couple of minutes.

Increase the heat to medium-high & add the chicken pieces, let simmer for 7 minutes, until no longer pink in the middle. Stir in the cabbage & cook for 3 minutes, until wilted. Remove the soup immediately from heat and stir in the fish sauce and lime juice. Serve hot and enjoy.

Red Curry Tofu Soup

Feel free to serve it with some lemon wedges on the side. Increase the heat of this soup with a pinch or two of black pepper.

Ingredients

1 package extra firm tofu (12 oz.), drained & cubed

2 cups vegetable broth

1 can coconut milk (14 oz.)

2 stalks lemon grass, bruised & chopped

½ teaspoon Thai red curry paste

5 makrut lime leaves, torn in half

½ cup shiitake mushrooms, stemmed & sliced

2 tablespoons lime juice, fresh

1 piece galangal (1")

½ cup button mushrooms, sliced

2 ½ tablespoons brown sugar

½ teaspoon red pepper flakes, crushed

4 oz. rice stick noodles, dry

⅛ teaspoon turmeric powder

Directions

Bring broth with coconut milk, lemon grass, lime leaves and galangal to a simmer over moderate heat in a large pot. Let simmer for 12 to 15 minutes, ensure that you don't bring the broth to come to a boil.

Strain the broth & discard the solids. Once done, immediately whisk in the red curry paste and add the tofu followed by button mushrooms, shiitake mushrooms, lime juice, turmeric, and brown sugar to the soup. Continue cooking for 10 more minutes, until mushrooms have softened.

In the meantime, fill a large pot with lightly salted water and bring it to a boil, over moderate heat. Add and cook the rice stick noodles until tender, for 3 to 5 minutes, drain well.

Place the drained noodles into bowls and then, ladle the hot soup on top of the noodles. Just before serving, garnish each bowl with the crushed red pepper flakes. Serve hot and enjoy.

Spicy Thai Vegetable Soup

Absolutely delicious and light to digest! If you are unable to find Thai chiles, then you can always use jalapeno and lemon grass with lemon zest.

Ingredients

3 tablespoons fish sauce

1 cup brown rice, uncooked

3 tablespoons olive oil

1 sweet onion, chopped

4 garlic cloves, minced

¼ cup fresh ginger root, chopped

2 tablespoons soy sauce

1 cup carrots, chopped

4 cups broccoli, chopped

1 red bell pepper, diced

3 Thai chile peppers

1 can light coconut milk (14 oz.)

6 cups vegetable broth

1 cup white wine

2 tablespoons fresh lemon grass, chopped

1 tablespoon Thai pepper garlic sauce

¾ cup plain yogurt

1 teaspoon saffron

2 cups water

fresh cilantro, for garnish

Directions

Bring the water and rice to a boil over moderate heat in a large pot. Decrease the heat, cover & let simmer for 40 to 45 minutes.

Next, over moderate heat in a large pot, heat up the olive oil until hot & cook the onion with ginger, garlic, and carrots until tender, for 5 minutes.

Mix in the red bell pepper, broccoli, Thai chile peppers, coconut milk, wine, broth, soy sauce, fish sauce, garlic sauce, saffron and lemon grass, let simmer for 25 minutes.

Work in batches and pour the soup into a food processor or blender, blend until completely smooth & creamy. Add soup to the pot again & mix in the cooked rice and yogurt. Just before serving, top your soup with the cilantro. Enjoy.

Thai Hot and Sour Soup

Once you prepare this soup, you will make it again. You can serve the same with almost anything, like noodles, rice and so on.

Ingredients

2 skinless, boneless chicken breast halves - shredded

1 tablespoon tom yum paste

3 cups chicken stock

1 tablespoon fish sauce

3 stalks lemon grass, chopped

1 tablespoon fresh lime juice

4 oz. fresh mushrooms, sliced thinly

1 teaspoon green chile pepper, chopped

½ garlic clove, finely chopped

A bunch of fresh coriander, chopped

2 makrut lime leaves

A sprig of fresh basil, chopped

Directions

Over moderate heat in a large saucepan, bring the chicken stock to a boil. Stir in the garlic and tom yum paste, cook for two minutes. Stir in the lime leaves and lemon grass. Place the chicken in the saucepan & cook until juices run clear and no longer pink, for 5 minutes.

Add the mushrooms & mix well. Add the green chile pepper, fish sauce, and lime juice. Continue to cooking & stir until blended well. Remove from the heat, serve warm with the basil and coriander.

Thai Red Curry Soup

This recipe is famous in several parts of Thailand. For a healthier meal, feel free to serve this soup with another protein packed recipe. Enjoy.

Ingredients

18 large shrimp, peeled & deveined

1 large red bell pepper, diced

2 tablespoons olive oil, divided

1 medium onion, diced

3 garlic cloves, minced

1 tablespoon fresh ginger, grated

3 tablespoons red curry paste

1 can light coconut milk (13.5 oz.)

4 cups chicken stock, unsalted

1 pouch Jasmine rice (8.8 oz.)

3 green onions, thinly sliced

¼ cup each of fresh cilantro leaves and basil leaves, chopped

2 teaspoons brown sugar

1 tablespoon lime juice, fresh

2 teaspoons fish sauce

¼ teaspoon each of ground black pepper, and kosher salt

Directions

Over moderate heat in a large Dutch oven, heat up 1 tablespoon of olive oil until hot. Season the shrimp with pepper and salt to taste. Add shrimp to the hot pot & cook until pink, for 2 to 3 minutes, turning halfway & set aside.

Add the leftover olive oil with onion, bell pepper & garlic to the hot pot. Cook until tender, for 3 minutes, stirring occasionally. Stir in the ginger and curry paste. Cook until fragrant, for a minute.

Stir in the coconut milk, stock & rice, scraping down any browned bits.

Bring the mix to a boil. Once done, decrease the heat & cook for 8 to 10 minutes, until reduced, stirring occasionally. Stir in the brown sugar and fish sauce. Remove from the heat.

Puree the soup in pot using an immersion blender until pureed. Add soup to the pot again.

Stir in basil, cilantro, green onions & lime juice. Evenly divide the soup among six bowls & top each bowl with 3 pieces of shrimp. Serve immediately and enjoy.

Creamy Carrot with Curry Soup

One of the best soup recipes that I have ever prepared! You can add a bit of chili to make it a bit spicy. Feel free to serve it with coleslaw and enjoy. Delicious!

Ingredients

1 ½ pounds carrots, peeled & cut into 1" chunks

2 tablespoons olive oil

1 large onion, cut into large dice

3 large garlic cloves, thickly sliced

1 tablespoon butter

2 tablespoons curry powder

A pinch of sugar

3 cups chicken broth

Freshly ground pepper & salt, to taste

1 ½ cups half-and-half (or whole milk)

Garnish: Roasted pistachios, chopped

Directions

Over moderate heat in a large, deep sauté pan, heat up the oil until shimmering hot.

Add carrots followed by the onion, sauté for 7 to 8 minutes, until vegetables begin to turn golden brown, stirring occasionally.

Decrease the heat to low & add butter, garlic and sugar, continue cooking for 10 more minutes, until all vegetables turn spotty caramel in color.

Add the curry powder & continue to sauté for a minute, until fragrant.

Add broth, bring the mix to a simmer. Once done, decrease the heat to low & let simmer for 10 minutes, until carrots are tender, partially covered.

Puree everything together using an immersion blender for half a minute, until very smooth.

Pour the soup back to the soup pot, add half-and-half until you get soup like thick consistency. Taste & season with pepper and salt, if required. Heat through & ladle into individual bowls then, garnish & serve. Enjoy.

Wonton Soup

Absolutely crunchy & delicious! You will ask for more, once you try it. You can even add a bit of garlic water and vinegar to this soup.

Ingredients

For Wontons:

1 teaspoon rice wine vinegar

2/3 pound ground pork

1 teaspoon ginger, freshly grated

2 teaspoons chives, thinly sliced

1 garlic clove

½ teaspoon red pepper flakes

1 teaspoon cornstarch

½ teaspoon toasted sesame oil

1 tablespoon soy sauce, reduced-sodium

¼ cup water

1 package square wonton wrappers

For Soup:

4 cups chicken broth, reduced-sodium

1 piece ginger (2"), peeled

2 garlic cloves, smashed

1 tablespoon soy sauce, reduced-sodium

2 tablespoons scallions, thinly sliced, for garnish

¼ teaspoon toasted sesame oil

Directions

Combine the pork with garlic, vinegar, chives, soy sauce, ginger, cornstarch, oil, and red pepper flakes in a large-sized mixing bowl until incorporated well.

Wet the edges of your wonton wrapper with a bit of water using your finger. Place approximately half a tablespoon of the prepared pork filling in middle of wonton wrapper. Fold the wonton diagonally into half and create a triangle, seal the edges & fold the two identical corners in on each other, pressing again to seal. Repeat until you have filled the all wonton wrappers are filled.

Bring the soup ingredients to a boil, over moderate heat. Let simmer for 10 minutes, on low-heat and then remove garlic cloves and ginger, bring it to a boil again. Lower in the wontons & cook for 8 to 10 more minutes.

Serve into individual bowls, garnished each with the scallions. Enjoy.

Egg Drop Soup

Absolutely delicious & tempting! For more heat, feel free to sprinkle a pinch or two of black pepper & red chili powder.

Ingredients

4 eggs, well beaten

1 tablespoon soy sauce, reduced-sodium

¼ teaspoon ground ginger

1 tablespoon cornstarch

6 cups chicken broth, low-sodium

1 teaspoon sesame oil

Freshly ground black pepper & kosher salt to taste

For Garnish:

2 tablespoons scallions, thinly sliced

Directions

In a large pot over medium heat, bring broth and ginger to boil. Whisk soy sauce and cornstarch together then whisk into broth.

Bring it to a boil and continue to cook for 3 minutes, until slightly thickened, then remove from the heat & immediately add the sesame oil.

Give it a good stir and then, pour in the eggs in a slow stream, ensure that you don't stir. Season with pepper and salt to taste.

Serve immediately, garnished with scallions and enjoy.

Miso Soup

You can increase the heat by adding crushed red chili flakes or by adding a few pinches of black pepper.

Ingredients

4 oz. silken tofu, cut into ½" cubes

1 large piece kombu (approximately 4")

2 tablespoons wakame, dried

1 ½ cups bonito flakes

3 tablespoons scallions, sliced, for garnish

1/3 cup white miso

6 cups water

Directions

For Dashi: Over moderate heat in a large pot, bring kombu & water to a simmer. As soon as the water begins to simmer, immediately remove the kombu. Bring the stock to a boil, over moderate heat.

Once done, add the bonito flakes and then, decrease the heat to a simmer. Continue to cook for 12 to 15 minutes. Strain the bonito flakes out, ensure that you press them to release any stock.

Return the dashi to stove & bring it to a simmer. Whisk in the miso until completely dissolved and then scallions and wakame.

Add some of the tofu cubes to the serving bowls and pour the hot soup carefully on top. Serve immediately and enjoy.

Ramen Chicken Noodle

Feel free to increase the heat by adding a pinch or two of red chili powder or black pepper. Serve this delicious soup recipe with flatbread or steamed cook rice and enjoy.

Ingredients

2 large carrots, peeled & chopped

¼ cup cilantro, freshly chopped

3 garlic cloves, minced

4 cups chicken broth, low-sodium

2 packages ramen noodles (seasoning packets discarded)

1 tablespoon extra-virgin olive oil

2 bell peppers, chopped

Freshly ground black pepper & kosher salt to taste

2 cups rotisserie chicken, shredded

½ cup green onions, thinly sliced

Juice of 1 lime, plus lime wedges for serving

Directions

Over moderate heat in a large soup pot, heat up the oil until hot. Add the bell peppers with garlic, carrots, and green onions, season with pepper and salt to taste. Cook for 6 to 8 minutes, until soft.

Add in the chicken broth, bring the mix to a simmer, over moderate heat. Add the ramen noodles & continue to cook for 2 to 3 minutes, until tender and then stir in the chicken followed by lime juice, and cilantro. Let simmer until heated through. Serve hot with the lime. Enjoy.

Coconut Curry Cauliflower Soup
with Toasted Pepitas

Once you prepare this recipe, I am sure that you will make it again. Absolutely delish! Pepita's add crunch to this soup. Enjoy.

Ingredients

1 cup yellow onion, chopped

¼ cup toasted pepitas

1 teaspoon fresh ginger, peeled & chopped

2 garlic cloves, chopped

1 large cauliflower head, cut into small florets

32 oz. vegetable broth, low-sodium

1 cup coconut milk, full-fat (shake well)

2 tablespoons red curry paste

1 cup carrots, chopped

¼ cup fresh cilantro, chopped

1 teaspoon extra-virgin olive oil

Flaky sea salt

1 teaspoon kosher salt

Directions

Over low heat in a small skillet, dry toast the pepitas for 2 minutes, until golden brown, set aside.

Next, over medium to low heat in a large pot, heat up the olive oil until hot. Once done, add the garlic followed by onion, ginger, carrots & salt. Continue to cook for a couple of more minutes.

Add the cauliflower followed by coconut milk, curry paste and broth. Stir well & bring the mix to a boil. Decrease the heat and let simmer for 17 to 20 minutes and then, blend the soup using an immersion blender until completely smooth.

Garnish with the cilantro, toasted pepitas & flaky sea salt. Serve hot and enjoy.

Coconut Curry Pumpkin Soup

Absolutely delicious, healthy and tempting! You can sub the chicken stock with vegetable stock.

Ingredients

1 small onion, finely chopped

2 teaspoons fresh ginger, grated or

1 teaspoon ground ginger

1 ½ teaspoons cinnamon

2 teaspoons curry powder

1 teaspoon nutmeg

½ teaspoon cloves

1 garlic clove, minced

4 cups chicken stock

¼ cup brown sugar, packed

3 cups pumpkin puree (canned or fresh)

1 can coconut milk (14 oz.)

2 tablespoons extra-virgin olive oil

Freshly ground black pepper & kosher salt to taste

For Garnish:

Cilantro leaves

Toasted pumpkin seeds

Directions

Over moderate heat in a large pot, heat up the oil until hot. Add and cook the onion for 4 to 5 minutes, until tender. Add ginger and garlic, continue to cook for a minute, until fragrant, stirring frequently. Stir in the curry, nutmeg, cinnamon & cloves then, season with pepper and salt to taste.

Stir in the brown sugar and pumpkin puree then whisk in the vegetable stock, bring it to a boil. Once done, decrease the heat & let simmer for 15 minutes, until thickened slightly.

Add the coconut milk & continue to cook until warmed through, over low heat then season with pepper and salt.

Serve in bowls, garnished with cilantro and toasted pumpkin seeds.

Thai Chicken & Corn Chowder

Absolutely delicious, healthy and a perfect recipe for guests! Enjoy this soup hot on a cold day.

Ingredients

2 large potatoes, peeled & cut into cubes, preferably 1.5cm

1 tablespoon sunflower oil

2 corn cobs, fresh, kernels removed using a small sharp knife

1 can coconut milk (400ml)

2 tablespoons green curry paste, gluten-free

½ cup chicken stock

2 chicken breast fillets, cut into thin strips

Juice & zest of 1 large lime, fresh

2 teaspoons fish sauce or to taste

2 kaffir lime leaves

To Serve:

Sliced chili, coriander leaves & Thai basil

Directions

Steam the corn kernels and chopped potato over a saucepan filled with boiling salted water until the potato is just tender, for 3 to 5 minutes.

Next, heat up the oil over moderate heat in a large saucepan until hot. Add and cook the curry paste until fragrant, for 30 seconds, stirring. Stir in the chicken, stock, coconut milk, lime juice and zest, and kaffir lime leaves, let simmer for 2 to 3 minutes, until chicken is completely cooked through.

Add the corn and potato, cook for a minute or two. Season with the fish sauce to taste

Once done, ladle the chowder into warm bowls, serve topped with the sliced chili, coriander and basil leaves.

Coconut Curry Butternut Squash Soup

Absolutely delicious & healthy! Feel free to serve this delicious soup with Indian Na'an or topped with breadcrumbs.

Ingredients

1 small yellow onion, diced

2 garlic cloves, minced

2 cups chicken or vegetable broth

1 butternut squash, medium-sized, peeled, seeded & cut into 1″ cubes

2 tablespoons Thai red curry paste

1 can coconut milk (15 oz.), divided

1 teaspoon ginger, freshly grated

¼ teaspoon freshly ground pepper, plus more to taste

Juice of 1 lime

1 tablespoon canola oil

½ teaspoon salt, plus additional to taste

For Garnish:

1/3 cup unsalted, dry-roasted peanuts, chopped

1/3 cup fresh cilantro, chopped

Optional Ingredients:

Naan, to serve

Sriracha to taste

Directions

Over moderate heat in a large soup pot, heat up the oil until hot. Add in the onion and garlic, sauté for 2 to 3 minutes, until soft & fragrant. Add the ginger & curry paste, give the ingredients a good stir until mixed well with the garlic and onion. Cook for 2 to 3 minutes more, stirring every now and then.

Add the cubes of butternut squash & slowly pour in the broth, give the ingredients a good stir until mixed well. Season with pepper and salt to taste, bring the mix to a boil, over moderate heat. Once done, decrease the heat to a simmer, cover & cook until butternut squash is just tender, for 20 minutes. Remove from the heat & let cool for a couple of minutes.

Work in batches & pour the prepared soup into a blender, blend until completely smooth.

Just before serving, remove the pureed soup from heat & mix in the coconut milk (reserving a few spoons) & lime juice, mix well. Season with more of pepper and salt. For extra spice, feel free to add sriracha to taste. Pour into individual bowls & drizzle with the kept-aside coconut milk. Swirl using a large spoon. Sprinkle with chopped peanuts and chopped cilantro. Serve warm and enjoy.

Healthy Fish & Pumpkin Soup

You will fall in love with this delicious soup recipe. Absolutely delish! This is a very famous recipe in Thailand and often served with breads as their regular meal.

Ingredients

3 tablespoons of Thai red curry paste

2 tablespoons of tamarind puree

250g pumpkin, peeled, cut into 2cm pieces

2 tablespoons fish sauce

600g skinless chunky fish fillets, cut into 3cm pieces

1 tablespoon brown sugar

4 Asian (red) eschalots, thinly sliced

1 green capsicum, cut into strips

1 tablespoon sunflower oil

3 cups chicken or fish stock (750ml), low-salt

1 can light coconut milk (200ml)

1 long red chili, thinly sliced

100g baby spinach leaves

2 kaffir lime leaves, finely shredded

Directions

Over moderate heat in a large saucepan, heat up the oil until hot. Once done, add & cook the curry paste until turns fragrant, for a minute or two, stirring frequently.

Next, add the stock followed by eschalot, coconut milk, kaffir lime leaves and chili, give the mix a nice stir until mixed well. Add the pumpkin followed by fish sauce, tamarind, capsicum, sugar and a pinch of salt, continue to cook until the pumpkin turns tender, for 17 to 20 minutes.

Add the pieces of fish & let simmer until turn opaque, for a couple of minutes.

Place half of the spinach into four warm bowls & top each bowl with the vegetable and fish.

Scatter with the leftover spinach and then, ladle the sauce on top, serve immediately and enjoy.

Potato Soup with Indian Spices

Absolutely delish! Surely one of the best soups that I have ever prepared! The best part about this soup is that you can refrigerate the leftovers for up to 3 days. Upon re-heating, just add a bit of water and serve it with flat breads/chapattis.

Ingredients

For Soup

2 tablespoons butter, unsalted

1 teaspoon turmeric powder

2 pounds Yukon Gold potato, cut into 1" chunks

1 tablespoon fresh ginger, grated

3 carrots, medium, diced

¼ teaspoon cayenne powder

3 stalks of celery, diced

½ teaspoon asafetida (optional)

2 medium onions, diced

Kosher salt, to taste

For Garnish:

¼ cup cilantro, roughly chopped

Lime wedges

For Tarka

1 small green chile, chopped

2 tablespoons neutral oil or ghee

1 teaspoon cumin seeds

4 garlic cloves, minced

½ teaspoon black mustard seeds

Directions

Over moderate heat in a heavy-bottomed soup pot, heat up the butter until melted. Once done, immediately add the onions and a bit of salt, cook for 6 to 8 minutes, until softened & turn brown, stirring frequently. Add celery and carrots, cook for 5 more minutes.

Add turmeric, asafetida, cayenne and ginger, give the ingredients a good stir until nicely coated & cook for a minute more. Add the potato chunks with 6 cups of water, bring it to a boil, over moderate heat. Decrease the heat & maintain a brisk simmer.

Add a pinch of salt, continue to cook for 15 minutes, until potatoes are soft. Taste broth, adjust the amount of salt & heat as required. Feel free to add ¼ teaspoon of cayenne should to the soup and make it fairly spicy.

Crush some of the potatoes using a potato masher and continue to cook for 5 more minutes, until the soup is slightly thickened. Turn the heat off.

For Tarka: Over moderate heat in a small skillet, heat up the ghee but don't let it turn too hot. Decrease the heat, add the garlic & cumin seeds, stir well. Cook for a minute or two, until cumin seeds have started to turn brown, and garlic is colored barely, stirring frequently. Add green chile and mustard seeds. When mustard seeds start to pop, add this tarka to the hot soup & stir well.

Ladle the hot soup carefully into individual bowls & garnish each bowl with cilantro. Serve immediately and enjoy.

Mulligatawny Soup

You will fall in love with this delicious soup. You can even add your favorite veggies to this soup and can serve it hot on a cold day.

Ingredients

1 tablespoon fresh curry, chopped

4 garlic cloves, minced

1 medium to large apple, peeled, cored & chopped

2 teaspoons fresh ginger, grated

1 medium onion, chopped

2 green chile peppers, chopped

1 cup red lentils (Masoor dhal), rinsed, drained

¼ teaspoon ground cinnamon

1 ½ teaspoons ground cumin

1 carrot, chopped

¼ teaspoon ground cloves

1 tablespoon lemon juice

2 teaspoons ground coriander seed

1 teaspoon ground turmeric

4 pods cardamom, bruised

1 large potato, peeled & diced

8 cups chicken broth

1 tablespoon tamarind concentrate

2 cups coconut milk

1 tablespoon vegetable oil, or clarified butter (ghee)

2 tablespoons chopped fresh cilantro

Directions

Over low heat in a large pan, heat up the vegetable oil or ghee until melted and hot

Once done, add & cook the onion with garlic, chilies, ginger, curry leaves and spices until mixture is fragrant & onion is lightly browned, stirring frequently, ensure that you don't over brown the onion.

Add apple with carrot, dhal, potato & chicken stock to the pan, bring the mix to a simmer. Cover & cook until vegetables are just tender, for 15 minutes, discarding the curry leaves and cardamom pods.

Work in batches & blend the soup mixture until pureed well then, add it back to the pan. Add coconut milk, lemon juice, tamarind & fresh coriander leaves, give it a good stir and continue to cook until heated through.

Indian Tomato Soup (Rasam)

This recipe is very famous in southern parts of India. People often prepare and serve it on special occasions and get together. Feel free to serve it as a dipping broth for fritters or as an appetizer.

Ingredients

3 pounds ripe, plump tomatoes, roughly puréed or cut into small dice

1 green chile (Serrano), sliced

2 teaspoons amchoor, divided

A pinch of asafoetida

4 garlic cloves, minced

1 tablespoon raw or dark brown sugar

2 teaspoons coriander seeds, ground

½ teaspoon charnushka

1 teaspoon sweet paprika

2 teaspoons black mustard seeds

1 teaspoon cumin seeds

3 tablespoons vegetable oil or ghee

Salt

8 curry leaves

Cilantro, for garnish

Directions

Over moderate heat in a soup pot, heat up the oil or ghee until it shimmers. Once done, immediately add in the mustard seeds, cook until they start to pop.

Once done, add the wet spices, give the ingredients a good stir until nicely coated with the oil.

Add the dry spices after a couple of seconds, stir again to coat. Once you can smell the aromatic, immediately add the tomatoes.

Bring the soup to a boil, over moderate heat. Once done, decrease the heat to a moderate simmer.

Cook roughly for half an hour, tasting often. Feel free to add sugar, salt or water, as required.

Just before serving, stir in the leftover amchoor & garnish the soup with cilantro. Enjoy.

Carrot Ginger Soup

This recipe is packed with essential nutrients and helps me stay full for a long period of time. Absolutely delicious! If you are serving this soup to toddlers or small kids, then you can omit using black pepper and can use less amount of ginger.

Ingredients

3 juicy red carrots, medium to large-sized, rinsed, peeled and chopped into cubes or small pieces

1 tablespoon ginger, peeled, rinsed & chopped

¼ teaspoon crushed black pepper or ground black pepper

1 tablespoon butter or olive oil

60 grams onion or ⅓ cup onions, peeled, chopped & rinsed

1 to 2 tablespoons fresh herbs, chopped such as mint, coriander, parsley, dill leaves,thyme or chives for garnish

2 cups vegetable stock or normal water or as needed

Salt, to taste

Directions

Over moderate heat in a large pan or saucepan, heat up the olive oil until hot. Once done, add the chopped onions & sauté until softened & turn translucent, on medium to low heat, stirring often.

Add and sauté the chopped ginger until you cannot smell any raw aroma of ginger, for 12 to 15 seconds.

Next, add the chopped carrots & season with salt to taste.

Continue to sauté and mix the carrots for a minute.

Add a cup of vegetable stock or water, give the ingredients a good stir until mixed well.

Using a lid, cover the pan & let simmer until the carrots are softened and fork tender, on medium to low heat.

Once you are done with the carrots, switch the heat off & place the pan on the kitchen countertop for a couple of minutes.

Next, add everything together in a blender jar or grinder. Add approximately ½ cup of stock/water & blend or grind until you get smooth & fine puree. Ensure that the puree is chunks free.

Add the pureed carrot mixture to the pan again.

Add ½ cup of veg stock / water more & mix well.

Cook on low heat until hot or warm and then, sprinkle with the ground black pepper, mix well.

Ladle the prepared soup into individual soup bowls & garnish each bowl with any fresh herb of your choice such as chives, coriander, parsley, mint, thyme or dill leaves.

Pepper Milagu Rasam

Absolutely delicious, healthy and quite easy to prepare! This recipe is very famous in the southern part of India. Serve this delicious soup recipe as it is or accompanied with rice, dosa or sambar. Enjoy.

Ingredients

1 ½ teaspoons tamarind, soaked in ½ cup of warm water & squeeze to get the pulp, strain & set aside

2 dry red chili, halved & seeded

1 tomato, chopped

8 garlic cloves

1 cup water

¼ cup fresh cilantro leaves

1 ½ teaspoons each of black pepper & cumin

1 teaspoon mustard seeds

8 curry leaf

1/8 teaspoon turmeric powder

1 tablespoon vegetable oil

Salt to taste

Directions

Add garlic with red chilies, cumin seeds and black pepper to a grinder. Grind until you get semi fine texture like consistency.

Next, over moderate heat in a large, non-stick skillet, heat up the oil until hot. Cook the mustard seeds for 30 seconds, until start to sizzle. Add the coarsely ground spices and curry leaves.

Sauté the mix for a minute, mix well. Add chopped coriander leaves and turmeric powder, give the ingredients a good stir until mixed well.

Add the chopped tomatoes followed by water and tamarind pulp. Season with salt to taste. Stir & let the rasam to simmer on a low heat for 12 to 15 minutes, until the tomatoes soften, without a lid. Serve hot and enjoy

Haddi Ka Shorba

Absolutely delish! You can serve this delicious soup on the dinner table with a chicken recipe, bread or even steamed rice and enjoy.

Ingredients

3 onions, large

1 ¼ pounds mutton bones, washed & cleaned

4 large tomatoes, blanched & finely chopped

1 ½ tablespoons grated ginger

2 teaspoons crushed pepper

1 ½ tablespoons Tur Dal

2 teaspoons cumin powder

½ teaspoon turmeric

6 to 7 tablespoons fresh coriander finely chopped

1 ½ tablespoons garlic, crushed

2 tablespoons ghee

Salt to taste

Directions

Over moderate heat in a large, pressure pan, heat up the ghee until melted and then, add the onions followed by garlic and ginger, fry until onions turn translucent, for a couple of minutes. Add tur dal followed by cumin powder, pepper powder, turmeric powder, chopped tomatoes, mutton bones, half of chopped coriander & 3 glasses of water then, sprinkle with salt to taste.

Close the lid, decrease the heat to low & cook for a whistle, for half an hour. Remove from heat and wait for 10 minutes so that the pressure releases naturally. Carefully remove the lid from your pressure pan.

Taste for cumin, pepper & salt, feel free to adjust the amount to your likings and cook for a minute or two more.

Just before serving, garnish with the leftover coriander leaves. Serve hot and enjoy.

Delicious Mutton Soup

Absolutely delicious and quite easy to prepare! The best part about this soup is that you can serve it almost with anything you want.

Ingredients

1 ¼ pounds mutton with bones, cleaned & washed

½ teaspoon turmeric powder

4 green chilies

½ teaspoon garlic-ginger paste

2 onions, medium size, finely sliced

¼ teaspoon black pepper powder

3 tablespoons coriander leaves, chopped

1 tablespoon olive oil

5 black pepper corns

Salt to taste

3 cups of water

Directions

Over moderate heat in a pressure cooker, heat up the oil until hot and then, add the pieces mutton with bones.

Add sliced onions followed by turmeric powder, coriander leaves, green chilies, ginger garlic paste, black pepper corns & salt to taste.

Mix well & cook for 10 to 12 minutes, over moderate heat, stirring frequently.

Add water & give it a good stir.

Taste & feel free to add more of salt to taste.

Cover the pressure cooker with a lid.

Pressure cook for 5 to 6 whistles, until tender.

Switch the flame off. Wait for 10 minutes and then release any steam.

Remove the lid & cook uncovered on low flame for 5 minutes.

Just before serving, sprinkle with the black pepper powder & garnish with chopped coriander leaves, serve hot and enjoy.

Sri Lanka Malu Soup

Absolutely delish! Feel free to serve this delicious soup with chapattis or steamed cook rice on the side and enjoy.

Ingredients

½ pound fish fillet, washed & cleaned

2 onions, chopped

1 curry leaves

50 grams lentils

½ teaspoon coriander

1 tomato, chopped

25 grams clarified butter (ghee)

1 teaspoon cumin

2 teaspoons lime juice

1 liter water

¼ teaspoon white pepper

Directions

Cook the fish in a large pan with half of the onion, lentils, tomato, coriander, pepper, cumin and water, over moderate heat.

Cook for 45 minutes and then, blend & strain the liquid.

Next, over moderate heat, heat up the ghee until melted & stir fry the leftover onion & curry leaves

Add this mix to the prepared fish soup & just before serving don't forget to sprinkle your soup with the lime juice. Serve hot and enjoy.

Sri Lankan Chicken Sodhi

Absolutely delicious and healthy! The most flavorful soup I have ever tried for my loved ones.

Feel free to serve it over steamed cooked basmati rice and enjoy.

Ingredients

1 onion, chopped

2 tablespoons tamarind pulp, undiluted

½ pound chicken bones, rinsed well

20 curry leaves

1 liter water

3 tablespoons black pepper

½ liter coconut milk

12 garlic cloves

Directions

Place the chicken bones in a large pot with tamarind, onion, curry leaves, and water. Stir well & bring it to a boil, let simmer for an hour.

Add the coconut milk & continue to cook for 5 more minutes.

In the meantime, crack the pepper using a mortar and then, add the garlic, continue to grind until you get rough paste like consistency.

Incorporate the paste into soup & sprinkle with salt to taste. Cook until it starts to boil, serve hot and enjoy.

Chicken and Sweet Corn Soup

Absolutely delish! Feel free to serve this delicious recipe on a cold winter night and enjoy the taste. Just before serving, top each serving with finely chopped lemon grass & red pepper flakes or black pepper.

Ingredients

200 g boneless, skinless chicken breast, finely shredded

5 g ginger, chopped

40 g Knorr Professional chicken seasoning powder

10 g garlic, chopped

300 g cream style sweet corn

50 ml prepared corn starch

5 Egg whites, slightly beaten

20 ml light soya sauce

50 ml vegetable oil

2 liters water

30 g thinly sliced Spring onions to garnish

Directions

Over low heat in a deep pan, heat up the oil, gently cook the chicken, ginger and garlic for a couple of minutes.

Blend the sweet corn, water, Knorr Chicken Seasoning Powder and soya sauce.

Bring the mix to a boil, add corn starch & gently simmer for a couple of minutes, stirring continuously.

Slowly drip egg whites into the soup pan, stirring with a chopstick or fork to form egg strands.

Season with salt to taste & then, garnish with the spring onions.

Green Pea Soup

Absolutely delicious and healthy! This soup recipe is a hit and a perfect way to keep yourself satiated and warm during the bone-chilling season.

Ingredients

1 medium onion, finely chopped

2 sprigs of fresh mint

1 cup peas

4 garlic cloves, chopped

½ cup milk

Salt to taste

Directions

Boil the peas, set aside to cool down at room temperature & preserve the water.

Next, over moderate heat in a large pan, sauté the onions and garlic until soft & brown, for a couple of minutes.

Add the peas & continue to sauté for a couple of more minutes and then cool. Blend the mixture & prepare a puree.

Add milk with mint leaves & salt. Bring the blend to a boil. Ladle into individual cups and garnish each cup with cream and mint leaf. Serve hot with your favorite bread.

Spinach & Pea Soup

Absolutely delicious and healthy! Forget about the vitamins and minerals, this soup will keep you full for several hours.

Ingredients

2 bunches fresh spinach leaves, chopped roughly

½ teaspoon white pepper powder

1 cup green peas, shelled & boiled

1 ½ cups vegetable stock

1 medium onion, chopped

1 ½ cups milk

1 teaspoon oil

Salt to taste

Directions

Over moderate heat in a large, deep non stick pan, heat up the oil until hot. Add the chopped onion & sauté. Add the spinach & continue to sauté. Once done, add the green peas followed by white pepper powder and salt, continue to sauté for a minute or two.

Transfer into a mixer jar & let slightly cool then, add the vegetable stock & puree. Once done, transfer the pureed soup into the pan again, add milk & bring everything together to a boil, over moderate heat. Transfer to a large serving bowl, serve hot and enjoy.

Thupka

Feel free to serve them with low carbohydrate marinara or ranch dressings on the side and enjoy.

A very famous recipe all the way from Nepal!

Ingredients

13 oz. stewing pork meat

1 medium onion chopped

11 oz. lamb with bones

1 oz. ginger finely chopped

3 garlic cloves, finely chopped

1 teaspoon cumin seed

7 oz. Chinese rice noodles or egg noodles

¼ teaspoon turmeric

2 tablespoons fresh cilantro, finely chopped

1 cup carrots, julienned into matchsticks (approximately 4 oz.)

2 cups bok choy, chopped

1 cup daikon, julienned into matchsticks (approximately 4 oz.)

12 cups water

1 teaspoon Szechuan pepper

Scallion greens, chopped, for garnish

5 tablespoons oil

Salt to taste

Directions

Over moderate heat in a large pot, heat up 2 tablespoons of oil until hot and then, add the cumin seed.

Cook until they begin to change their color & turn fragrant. Once done, add the onion, garlic and ginger, sauté until softened and then, remove from the pot.

Add the leftover oil. Add the pieces of meat & fry until browned.

Add 6 cups of water followed by turmeric and Szechuan pepper, bring the mix to a boil.

Decrease the heat and let simmer, cook for 2 hours, on medium-low heat.

Add carrot followed by bok choy and daikon along with 2 cups of water.

Bring it to a boil again & cook for 15 more minutes.

Add 4 more cups of water & noodles. Cook for 5 more minutes.

Add cilantro & salt, to taste.

Once done, give the ingredients a good stir until mixed well & cook for a minute more.

Garnish with fresh scallion greens and enjoy.

Tomato Soup

A very famous recipe from India! Absolutely delish & healthy! Feel free to top your soup with breadcrumbs or serve it you're your favorite muffins on side. Enjoy.

Ingredients

2 pounds ripe tomatoes; washed & cut into quarters

1 medium onion

2 squirts of tomato purée (approximately 2 teaspoons)

1 small carrot

2 tablespoons olive oil

1 celery stick

2 liters/2 pints of hot vegetable stock

2 bay leaves

A good pinch of sugar

Directions

Peel 1 carrot and 1 onion; chop both of them into very small-sized pieces and then, roughly chop the stick of celery just like you chopped the carrot and onion.

Next, over moderate heat into a heavy-based, large-sized pan; heat up 2 tablespoons of olive oil. Once done, immediately add the onion, celery and carrot; mix well using a large wooden spoon. Cook the veggies for 10 minutes, until soft & faintly colored, on low heat, stirring frequently and ensure that they don't stick together.

Hold the pipe on top of the pan, add approximately 2 teaspoons of the tomato purée; give it a good stir sond ensure that the vegetables turn red. Add the chopped tomatoes and then, sprinkle with a pinch of sugar & a bit of black pepper.

Next, tear the bay leaves into pieces & add to the hot pan; give the ingredients a good stir until mixed well. Cover the pan with the lid & let the chopped tomatoes to stew until their juices flow nicely and shrink down, for 10 minutes, on a low heat; shaking the pan occasionally.

Slowly add the hot stock, stirring well. Increase the heat & wait until bubbling. Once done; decrease the heat to low & cover the pan with the lid. Gently cook for 25 to 30 minutes, giving a good stir a few times.

Remove the hot pan carefully from heat, remove the lid & let sit for a couple of seconds then remove the bay leaf pieces. Work in batches & blend the soup carefully until approximately three-quarters full. Puree until the soup is completely smooth. Fill a bowl with the puréed soup. Repeat the blending process with the leftover soup.

Pour the puréed soup into the hot pan again & reheat for a couple of more minutes, at medium heat, stirring occasionally. Taste & feel free to add a pinch of salt, plus additional sugar and pepper, if desired. Ladle into individual bowls; serve hot and enjoy.

Mixed Fruit Soup

This is just like rich custard. Absolutely delicious & healthy, packed with the essential nutrients and vitamins of fruits!

Ingredients

1 medium orange

4 cups unflavored, unsweetened plant-based milk

1 dragon fruit, peeled into ¾" cubes

2 tablespoons arrowroot powder

1 dash ground turmeric

2 teaspoons pure vanilla extract

1 medium apple, cored & cut into ½" pieces

½ cup sliced fresh strawberries

1 medium pear, cored & cut into ½" pieces

2 fresh kiwi, peeled & cut into ¾" cubes

1 cup red and/or green grapes, halved

½ cup pomegranate seeds

1 medium banana

½ cup fresh blueberries

1 piece stick cinnamon (1")

Pure maple syrup, to taste

Directions

Over moderate heat in a large pot or Dutch oven, combine the milk, arrowroot powder, pure vanilla extract, stick cinnamon, and ground turmeric, bring the mix to a boil over medium to low, stirring frequently. Let simmer until thickened slightly, for 5 to 10 minutes, uncovered. Let completely cool. Remove the stick cinnamon.

In the meantime, cut the orange into supremes. Slice the stem & bottom ends off using a small sharp knife. Stand the fruit on a flat end & slice off all the peel, pith, and outer membrane. Release the segments by slicing along the membranes on either side.

Add the orange supremes followed by apple, pear, green and/or red grapes, kiwi, dragon fruit, strawberries, pomegranate seeds, and blueberries to the soup. Cover the pot & refrigerate until the soup is cold, for an hour or two.

Just before serving, peel & cut the banana into ½" pieces. Add to the chilled soup. Sweeten with maple syrup to taste.

Spicy Watermelon Soup

You will fall in love with the color of this soup. Just before serving, feel free to top your soup with cream and fresh cilantro leave. Enjoy.

Ingredients

6 cups watermelon; chopped & deseeded

½ tablespoon chili flakes or to taste

2 tablespoons mint, fresh, chopped

1 tablespoon garlic-ginger paste

Olive oil, as required, to cook

Directions

Over moderate heat in a large pan; heat up a bit of olive oil until hot and then, sauté the garlicginger paste & chili flakes; set aside at room temperature to cool.

Next, puree the mint and watermelon in a food processor or blender until blended thoroughly. Add the prepared watermelon puree carefully into hot pan with the garlic- ginger & chili flakes; let simmer for a couple of minutes, until thickens a bit. Season to taste and then, let chill for an hour or two.

Feel free to add a few ice cubes to the soup or simply spoon some of the olive oil on top & serve immediately; garnished with a fresh sprig of mint.

Madras Curry Vegetable Soup

Absolutely delish! For more heat, you can add the Sriracha with Asian chili sauce. Serve this delicious soup with couscous or rice, or simply pair it with a vegetable rice biryani for a complete Indian meal.

Ingredients

1 cup broccoli florets, chopped

2 cups water

1 tablespoon olive oil

¼ onion, sliced

3 garlic cloves, minced

1 can coconut milk (approximately 12 oz.)

½ carrot, thinly sliced

1 tablespoon fresh cilantro, chopped

½ cup mushrooms, sliced

1 cup vegetable broth

2 teaspoons Madras curry powder

Juice of ½ lime, fresh

1 teaspoon kosher salt

Directions

Fill a small saucepan with 2 cups of water and bring it to a boil, over high heat. Add and cook the broccoli for a minute. Drain the broccoli well, set aside

Next, over moderate heat in a large skillet or medium saucepan, heat up the olive oil until hot & add the onions, sauté for a couple of minutes, until onions are just softened. Add the minced garlic followed by mushrooms, carrot & cooked broccoli, continue to cook for 2 more minutes

Add broth and coconut milk to the hot pan, stir until mixed well. Add lime juice, curry powder, and salt then slowly let the mixture to simmer for 5 minutes, ensure that you don't bring the soup to a boil

Remove from the heat, serve the soup with freshly chopped cilantro and enjoy.

Conclusion

In conclusion, this Asian cookbook offers a wealth of diverse and flavorful recipes, showcasing the rich culinary heritage of the Asian continent. From Stir-fry Veggie to soups, each dish is sure to tantalize your taste buds and bring a touch of the exotic to your kitchen. So why not take a culinary journey through Asia today and discover the delicious flavors that await you.

CPSIA information can be obtained
at www.ICGtesting.com
Printed in the USA
LVHW022110180323
741951LV00007B/381